Preface by John Marti...
Chief Executive of Waterways ...

The reopening of the ... Royal ... years of effort and wo... Special thanks must go to the Royal Canal Amenity Group and the Inland Waterways Association of Ireland for their long term commitment to the restoration.

Waterways Ireland has been responsible for the management and restoration of the Royal Canal since 2000 and has secured funding for the restoration project through the National Development Plan. I would particularly like to thank Éamon Ó Cuív, Minister for Community, Rural and Gaeltacht Affairs and his predecessor, Síle de Valera, for their commitment to this project and to the waterways in general. The restoration works have been undertaken by a direct labour force working in hand with an in-house technical engineering team and a number of specialist bridge construction contractors. The reopening of the Royal Canal comes at a time when boat ownership on the inland waterways and interest in exploring new waterway opportunities is at an all time high. The completion of the work on the Royal Canal will not only provide a new waterway experience for many people, but will also provide a new loop to many previous Royal or Grand Canal users – the opportunity to travel the 'new triangle' – the Royal Canal, the Grand Canal and a short section of the Shannon Navigation.

This 5th edition of the Guide to the Royal Canal is intended to not only equip the boater with the information they need but also to provide general information for other recreational users of the canal; walkers, anglers, cyclists and canoeists. The Guide has been produced in conjunction with the Inland Waterways Association of Ireland and the Royal Canal Amenity Group, with the kind assistance of the Central Fisheries Board, Irish Canoe Union, Fáilte Ireland and Walking Ireland.

Whatever activity you partake of, enjoy your time on the Royal Canal. Journey on the 18th century works through the 21st century island surrounding you and become part of a wonderful future for the Royal Canal.

Preface by Paul Garland
President of the Inland Waterways Association of Ireland

The Royal Canal started life as a major goods and passenger corridor from Dublin to the River Shannon. With the improving rail and road links the canal suffered a steady decline into dereliction like so many other waterways. Its history and construction are tangible links to our past and are physical markers in Ireland's economic and social development.

The Inland Waterways Association of Ireland is proud of our involvement in returning this piece of living heritage into a new role as a recreational waterway. I would particularly like to thank our members Ruth Delany and Ian Bath who played pivotal roles with the Royal Canal Amenity Group together with the late Eddie Slane and the communities along the path of the canal in progressing the restoration and recording the history of the canal. Ian must also be commended for his contribution in updating the maps and text of this new edition.

John McKeown and the entire team of Waterways Ireland must also be congratulated on the standard of workmanship they have achieved. The sympathetic restoration of the original works and the skills employed in new construction make this a project they can be proud of. The canal is open, use it, enjoy it, and spare a thought for the many boatmen who navigated it over the two hundred years of its life.

CONTENTS

PUBLISHED BY WATERWAYS IRELAND IN ASSOCIATION WITH INLAND
WATERWAYS ASSOCIATION OF IRELAND
©Copyright of Content: Waterways Ireland and Inland Waterways Association of Ireland
Copyright of Base Maps: ERA Maptec Ltd, 40 Lower O'Connell Street, Dublin 1; map content has
been added by Waterways Ireland and Inland Waterways Association of Ireland

ISBN 978-0-9564994-0-0

NAVIGATING THE ROYAL CANAL

Navigation Authority

The Royal Canal is managed by Waterways Ireland Eastern Regional Office which is located at: Floor 2 Block C, Ashtowngate, Navan Road, Dublin 15. Tel: +353 (0)1 868 0148. Fax: +353 (0)1 838 3647.

Full information regarding Waterways Ireland's role and responsibilities as the Navigation Authority for the Inland Waterways can be found by accessing the website at **www.waterwaysireland.org**

Queries can be directed by email to **info@waterwaysireland.org**

The Royal Canal

The main line of the canal is 145.6 km long. There are 46 locks, 10 of which are double chambered. There is also a sea lock where the canal joins the River Liffey in Dublin. The Summit Level (highest point along the canal) is approximately 94.3 m higher than the entry level at Spencer Dock.

The official numbering of the locks is from North Strand Road, Dublin (No. 1), to the lock at Richmond Harbour, Cloondara (No. 46) where the canal meets the Shannon Navigation. The Main Line of the canal from Spencer Dock to Cloondara is due to be reopened by 2010. There will still remain two obstructions to full navigation in Spencer Dock; the non-operational Spencer lifting bridge carrying Sheriff Street across the dock and a high-voltage electricity cable that crosses the canal at towpath level beside the bridge. Boaters will need to contact the Waterways Ireland Eastern Regional Office in advance of entering Spencer Dock.

Navigation Criteria

This navigation criteria is common to the Royal Canal, the Grand Canal Main Line and the Grand Canal Barrow Line.

- Length of locks   21 m
- Beam (width) of locks   3.9 m
- Draft   1.2 m
- Airdraft*   3 m

*(Lowest Bridge on the Royal Canal is the Liffey Junction Railway Bridge (bridge below 7th Lock)

Permits

Boats must display a valid Permit. Permits must be obtained from Waterways Ireland – they authorise lock passages and mooring. Boat users can either purchase an Annual Permit (which includes unlimited mooring and lock passages) or purchase monthly Mooring Permits and pay for lock passages on an individual basis. **All permits must be bought in advance.**

Moorings

Under the Canals Act (1986) Bye-Laws (1988), a boat can moor at the same public mooring or within 500 m of the same place for a maximum of 5 days.

Landing Jetties

Landing jetties are provided at locks or bridges to facilitate navigation through the area and are not for longer term mooring.

Traffic

The general rule is that traffic should keep to the right, but when navigation is clear ahead, travel towards the centre of the canal. Take extreme care and reduce speed appropriately when approaching bends and bridges etc. If the view of navigation ahead is blocked, keep to the right taking due recognition of the depths available. Some locations are narrow and should be navigated with care particularly when passing or overtaking other boats.

The Speed Limit on the Canal is 6 km/h.

Harbours/Slipways

There are slipways at:-

Confey, 12th level between Collins Bridge and Cope Bridge	(Map 2)
Maynooth Harbour	(Map 3)
Enfield Harbour	(Map 5)
Thomastown Harbour	(Map 7)
Mullingar Harbour	(Map 9)
Ballinea Harbour	(Map 10)
Ballynacargy Harbour	(Map 11)
Abbeyshrule	(Map 11)

There are also harbours at other locations as indicated on individual maps.

Dry Docks

There are dry docks at Mullingar Harbour and at Richmond Harbour, Cloondara. Permission to use a dock is obtainable from the Royal Canal Depot at Thomastown. Advance booking is essential.
Tel: +353 (0)44 937 4940.

Safety

Ensure that boats have sufficient crew to handle them effectively. In line with legislative requirements under S.I. 259/2004, Waterways Ireland advises all users of the navigation to wear a lifejacket at all times while on board. Ensure there are sufficient, suitable lifejackets on board for all boat passengers.

Lock chambers are not equipped with ladders or lifebuoys. Swimming is not allowed in any lock, harbour or dock.

Health

The quality of water in the canal is generally good but, unlike tap water, it is untreated and micro-organisms are naturally present. The risk of contracting illness (including Weil's Disease) is small, but you should take sensible precautions:-

- cover any cuts with a waterproof dressing;
- wash with clean water after canal activities;
- if you become ill within two weeks, let your doctor know that you have been in contact with untreated water.

Maps

The maps in this guide are based on the Ordnance Survey Permit No. 4179. The Royal Canal is covered by the Ordnance Survey 1:50,000 Discovery Series sheets 40, 41, 48, 49 and 50. Visit **www.osi.ie**

Bus Services

The information given is correct at the time of going to press. It should be noted that in more remote areas the services tend to be very infrequent, no more than one or two buses per day in each direction. Reference should be made to the Dublin Bus (**www.dublinbus.ie**) or Bus Éireann Expressway & Local Bus Timetables (**www.buseireann.ie**) for full information. There are also train services from major towns (**www.irishrail.ie**).

Further Reading

Ireland's Royal Canal 1789 – 2009, Ruth Delany & Ian Bath, Lilliput Press 2010.
The Royal Canal, Peter Clarke, Elo Publications, 1992.
Ireland's Inland Waterways, Ruth Delany, Appletree Press, 2004
Green and Silver, L.T.C.Rolt, Third edition published in 1993 by Athlone Branch IWAI. Includes a description of a voyage along the Royal Canal in 1946.

OPERATING LOCKS

Introduction

All the locks on the Royal Canal, with the exception of the sea lock at Spencer Dock, are operated manually and require a lock key. The process is outlined below but operating locks requires some guidance initially.

Boat owners interested in putting a boat on the canal should contact Waterways Ireland Eastern Regional Office to make the necessary arrangements. When assistance with boat movement is required thereafter, you should contact the appropriate Water Patroller for Locks 1-17 or 17-46 on either of the numbers noted below.

Observe the correct procedure when passing your boat through the lock. The inexperienced should use lock gear extremely cautiously: nothing should be done unless you understand the consequences. In good order, lock racks and gates do not need much force to operate.

Contact Numbers

Eastern Regional Office	+353 (0)1 868 0148
Royal Canal Depot, Thomastown	+353 (0)44 937 4940
Locks 1 – 17	+353 (0)87 248 5754
Locks 17 – 46	+353 (0)87 618 2104

Locks

LOCK NO.	RISE	LOCK NO.	FALL
Sea lock	Length 36.0 m x Width 7.6 m		
1	2.50 m rise	26	2.20 m fall
2 (double)	6.60 m rise	27	2.15 m fall
3 (double)	5.40 m rise	28	2.45 m fall
4 (double)	5.35 m rise	29	2.90 m fall
5 (double)	5.50 m rise	30	2.75 m fall
6 (double)	5.30 m rise	31	2.70 m fall
7	2.60 m rise	32	2.75 m fall
8	2.70 m rise	33	2.95 m fall
9	2.10 m rise	34	2.85 m fall
10 (double)	5.50 m rise	35	2.75 m fall
11 (double)	5.55 m rise	36	3.00 m fall
12 (double)	5.60 m rise	37	2.75 m fall
13	2.75 m rise	38	2.80 m fall
14	2.95 m rise	39	3.00 m fall
15	2.65 m rise	40	3.10 m fall
16 (double)	4.95 m rise	41	3.05 m fall
17 (double)	5.05 m rise	42	3.10 m fall
18	2.85 m rise	43	3.05 m fall
19	2.75 m rise	44	3.15 m fall
20	2.80 m rise	45	2.70 m fall
21	2.70 m rise	46	2.60 m fall
22	2.60 m rise		
23	2.65 m rise		
24	2.65 m rise		
25	2.60 m rise (Summit)		

Equipment

Operation of the lock gates requires a lock key. It is a crank about 45 cm long with a handle at right angles not less than 25 cm long. A hole 3 cm square with sides parallel to the handle will fit all rack spindles. Lock keys can be purchased from Waterways Ireland Eastern Regional Office and the Grand Canal Depot in Tullamore.

Movement through locks
(See Diagram for explanation of lock features)

Movement through locks requires the lock chamber to be filled or emptied by opening or closing gates and raising or lowering the sluices within those gates. This equalises the water level between the canal high level and canal low level. The lock key operates the sluices via a rack and pinion system.

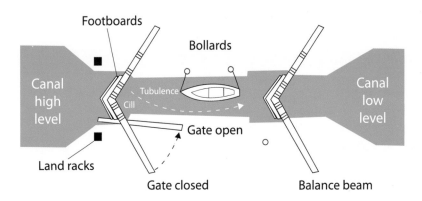

There are a number of different scenarios, depending on the direction of travel and on the position of the upper (breast) lock gates and the lower (tail) lock gates.

i)   Ascending when the lock chamber is empty

When the lock chamber is empty, the lower gates will be open.

With lower gates fully open, move boat into lock and ensure that the boat is well secured bow and stern using ropes and bollards, with crew ready to shorten the lines as the boat rises. Do not restrict the ability of the boat to move with the rising water.

Close lower gates ensuring that the mitred edges meet cleanly and then close all lower sluices.

Open upper sluice gently, a little at a time. Some turbulence will be generated when the first upper gate rack is raised so ropes should be tensioned or restrained, but not tied. The boat will tend to surge forward. It is best to raise the land tunnel racks first (if any) or the rack on the same side as the boat is tied, so that the surge of water does not tend to push the boat from the wall. Only when the turbulence eases off should a second rack be opened. Crew should also take care that no part of the boat is caught under any projection.

When water equalises, open upper gates and proceed.

ii) Ascending when the lock chamber is full

If the lock chamber is full, the lower gates and sluices will be closed. Close the upper gates ensuring that the mitred edges meet cleanly and then close all upper sluices.

Open lower sluices.

Open lower gates only when water equalises (not before) and move boat into the lock chamber.

Undertake step (i) as detailed on previous page.

iii) Descending when the lock chamber is full

If the lock chamber is full, the lower gates and sluices will be closed.

Move boat into the lock. Pass ropes around bollards, without tying them. Ropes should be fed through during the descent, allowing the boat to move with the falling water. Ensure that no part of the boat can catch on any projection as it falls. Particularly keep the rudder clear of the upper gates and of the cill under them.

Close the upper gates ensuring that the mitred edges meet cleanly and then close all upper sluices.

Open the lower sluices.

When water equalises, open the lower gates and proceed.

iv) Descending when the lock chamber is empty

If the lock chamber is empty, upper gates and sluices will be closed.

Close the lower gates ensuring that the mitred edges meet cleanly and then close all lower sluices.

Open upper sluices.

When water equalises, open upper gates and move boat into the lock.

Undertake step (iii) as detailed above.

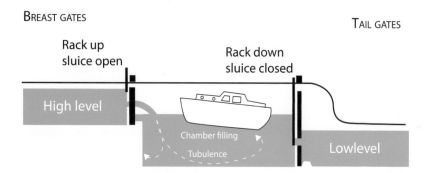

Sluice Operation

When raising sluices using the lock key (windlass), the safety catch (pawl) will automatically move from tooth to tooth on the rack and should not be released at any time during the lift.

When lowering sluices the pawl must be disengaged from the rack teeth by taking the weight of the sluice through raising the rack slightly to release the pawl. The control of the sluice is now maintained through the lock key and great caution should be exercised in lowering the sluice. At no stage should the sluice be allowed to lower or drop by releasing the lock key. In the final lowered position, re-engage the pawl.

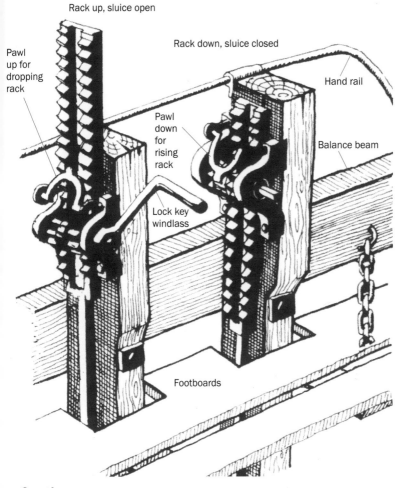

Rack up, sluice open

Pawl up for dropping rack

Rack down, sluice closed

Hand rail

Pawl down for rising rack

Balance beam

Lock key windlass

Footboards

Caution

DO NOT allow the sluice mechanism to lower under gravity, i.e. to simply drop without retaining control of the lock key. To do so may cause injury to person(s) or damage to the lock mechanism.

If in doubt, contact Waterways Ireland for assistance.

Operating a lock requires a certain amount of physical effort; please ensure that you are sufficiently fit to do so.

On no account should children (i.e. under the age of 16) be allowed to become involved in any of the lifting or lowering operations required during lock passage.

Beware of staying too close to the upper cill when descending.

Leaving Lock

The general rule is that unless another boat is about to use the lock, it is usual to leave the lock as it was, with the racks as you found them (i.e. if you found the lock full, leave it full).

Difficulties

Gates may jam with rubbish under them or fail to open completely due to rubbish lodging behind them. Re-opening or closing may help.

Man Overboard

Drop all racks at once and make the rescue from the boat. There are no ladders in the lock chambers.

Courtesy

While 'first come first served' is the rule, it is preferable to give priority to a boat coming down when the lock is full or to a boat ascending when the lock is empty. Enter the lock slowly.

FISHING ON THE ROYAL CANAL

The Central Fisheries Board (CFB) is a statutory body with responsibility for inland fisheries and sea angling operating under the aegis of the Department of Communications, Energy and Natural Resources. It was established under the Fisheries Act 1980. Waterways Ireland has commissioned the CFB to conduct scientific research aimed at understanding and improving habitat conditions for fish and aquatic life on the Royal Canal, Grand Canal (Main Line & Barrow Line), the Barrow Navigation and the Shannon-Erne Waterway. Allied to this research role, close attention is focused on the requirements of anglers as well as other waterways users. In the last six years (2003-2009), as part of this ongoing programme, in excess of 2.5 tonnes of coarse fish have been stocked into the Royal Canal.

The Royal Canal averages 12 m wide and is approximately 1.6 m deep. Water in the Royal Canal can be very clear, which can make day-time fishing difficult. Accordingly, angling is often most productive towards the hours of dawn and dusk. The canal corridor supports a wide diversity of aquatic and marginal plants that harbour myriads of fish-food insects. This may explain the large quantity of plump and well conditioned fish that are resident in the canal. The vegetation is carefully managed and does not pose an obstruction for anglers.

Fishing Tackle and Bait

For most fish species, pole tackle is the best fishing method on this relatively narrow canal. Float fishing can also be successful. Most anglers beginning a session should firstly target the middle of the canal, fishing the bait just on the bottom. It is advisable to introduce a small amount of groundbait at the start of the session (between four and eight small balls) and loose feed thereafter. It may be worth adding some extra groundbait if a number of cruisers pass. Fish with No. 6 or 8 elastic, 1.4 kg main line to a 0.9 kg hook length, and a medium-wire, size 18 hook. As a general rule the lighter the tackle the greater the catch. However, large fish patrol the canal and, if hooked, will test your equipment, so be prepared to introduce heavier terminal tackle. A wide range of hook baits work in this canal, although white and red maggot, pinkies, casters and worm often work best. It is worth having corn on standby, particularly if larger species are targeted.

Good pike fishing is available throughout the canal. A roving approach, continuously covering new water, should maximise sport. A wide range of techniques will work including dead-baits or artificial lures. Fly fishing for pike can also be productive and is becoming increasingly popular. Basic pike tackle incorporating suitable wire trace should be employed whatever method is used.

Further reading

Waterways Ireland Angling Guide provides concise information and maps of the superb fishing locations along the inland waterways. Available free of charge from Waterways Ireland. Visit **www.waterwaysireland.org**

Visit **www.cfb.ie**

BAITS: MAGGOTS, CASTERS,
BREAD, PASTE, SWEETCORN, WORMS.
SPECIMEN WEIGHT: 0.907 KG
IRISH RECORD: 1.425 KG

Roach are by far the most numerous fish species throughout the canal network, normally representing in excess of 70% of fish numbers. While roach are relative newcomers to many Irish canal fisheries they are now ubiquitous and form the basis of many match and pleasure fisheries. Roach can reach a maximum size of 2 kg and typically average between 50 to 100 g in weight. Good numbers of larger fish can be found along the canal. Roach are easily identified by their bright silver colouration, and their orangey red fins and eyes.

BAITS: MAGGOTS, WORMS, CASTERS,
SWEETCORN, BREAD, PASTE.
SPECIMEN WEIGHT: 3.402 KG
IRISH RECORD: 5.528 KG

Bream are traditionally one of the favourite fish species among canal anglers. A shoal fish, they can reach a maximum size of 7 kg, although in the canal a fish of 1 to 2 kg would be considered normal. Anglers targeting canal bream search for the areas of coloured water that signal the presence of feeding bream shoals. Adult bream are recognised by their bronze colour, black fins and protruding upper jaw. Young bream or 'skimmers' differ from adults due to their silver colouring.

BAITS: MAGGOTS, WORMS, CASTERS,
SWEETCORN, BREAD, PASTE.
SPECIMEN WEIGHT: 1.6 KG
IRISH RECORD: 3.175 KG

Roach x bream hybrids occur wherever the parent species coexist, but can also be found in the absence of bream. A hard fighting fish, they are a popular angling quarry. Intermediate in appearance between the parent species, large hybrids can be distinguished from bream by their shorter anal fin. Hybrids can weigh up to 4 kg, but a fish over 0.5 kg would be regarded as a good canal catch.

BAITS: MAGGOTS, CASTERS, SWEETCORN,
BREAD, PASTE, WORMS, MINI BOILIES.
SPECIMEN WEIGHT: 2.722 KG
IRISH RECORD: 3.697 KG

Tench are an increasingly popular angling quarry and are widespread throughout the canal network. Tench were first introduced to the Royal Canal by the Inland Fisheries Trust – a precursor to the Central and Regional Fisheries Boards, near Mullingar, in the 1960s. This area remains a premier tench fishery. Tell-tale fizzy bubbles on the surface of the water betray the presence of feeding tench to observant anglers. While tench can weigh up to 5 kg, the typical canal fish will weigh between 1 and 2 kg. An attractive fish, tench are a dark olive or blackish colour with rounded fins and an almost unforked tail. They have distinctive, bright red eyes.

BAITS: MAGGOTS, BREAD, CASTERS, SWEETCORN, PASTE, WORMS, FLIES.
SPECIMEN WEIGHT: 1.021 KG
IRISH RECORD: 2.041 KG

Rudd are widespread but are present in relatively low numbers throughout the canal network, having been largely out-competed by the closely related roach. While the rudd can attain a maximum size of 2.5 kg, canal fish average 50 to 100 g in weight. Rudd can be distinguished from roach by their generally more golden colour and more rounded appearance. The fins of rudd are a vivid red colour. They have a pronounced, protruding lower jaw that allows them to feed on the surface of the canal. They can frequently be spotted feeding at the surface on warm summer evenings.

BAITS: MAGGOTS, CASTERS, BOILIES, SWEETCORN, WORMS, BREAD, FISH NUTS
SPECIMEN WEIGHT: 5.443 KG
IRISH RECORD: 13.523 KG

Carp A 'specialists' fish species that is relatively uncommon in the canals. Carp can be fished for in certain isolated canal locations, although they can be difficult to catch. Carp are renowned as one of the hardest fighting freshwater fish. Reaching a maximum size of 14 kg, canal carp up to 10 kg have been reported. Fish of 4 to 5 kg are more typical. Two varieties of carp are present in the canals. These are the fully scaled common carp and the partially scaled mirror carp. Dull brown in colour, carp are a stocky muscular fish with an elongated dorsal fin. Four barbels on the large mouth help the carp detect food items on the canal bed.

BAITS: WORMS, MAGGOTS, CASTERS, SMALL DEAD FISH AND A RANGE OF SPINNING BAITS.
SPECIMEN WEIGHT: 1.2 KG
IRISH RECORD: 2.495 KG

Perch can be found in all canal fisheries. Reaching a maximum size of 3 kg, perch are aggressive, greedy feeders. They are rough and prickly to the touch and are easily recognised by the characteristic vertical dark stripes along their usually green flanks. Perch have two dorsal fins, the first of which is well armed with very sharp spines.

BAITS: RANGE OF DEAD BAITS, SPINNERS AND PLUGS (INCLUDING JERKBAITS) AND FLIES.
SPECIMEN WEIGHT: LAKE: 13.608 KG
RIVER: 9.072 KG, IRISH RECORD:
LAKE: 19.391 KG, RIVER: 19.051 KG

Pike are ubiquitous throughout the canal network. In exceptional circumstances pike weigh up to 20 kg and can grow up to 1.3 m in length. While the typical canal pike average 2 to 3 kg in weight, much larger specimens up to 10 kg are present. Pike are fish eaters and are perfectly designed to do so. The pike has a streamlined, torpedo shaped body, and its mottled olive green colour provides perfect camouflage. It has a cavernous mouth with rows of needle sharp, backward pointing teeth.

WALKING THE ROYAL CANAL

Introduction

The Royal Canal runs for some 145.6 km from the River Liffey at Dublin's North Wall to the Shannon at Cloondara, in Co.Longford. The towpath along the still water is a walkers' paradise, a perfect combination of built heritage blended with natural environment. Canal terrain is suitable for walking by people of virtually all ages and levels of fitness and, since the towpath parallels the water, the route is largely self-guiding, with many fascinating landmarks along the way.

The Royal Canal Way is presently waymarked as a National Waymarked Way between the 10th Lock at Ashtown and Abbeyshrule, with signposts at most road bridges. It is intended in due course to continue this waymarking along the remaining length of the canal from Abbeyshrule to Cloondara. Although the urban stretch from 1st Lock at Newcomen to the 10th Lock at Ashtown is not waymarked, the Royal Canal provides an ideal urban walkway and a different perspective on the city of Dublin.

Before you start

- Wear appropriate footwear and clothing – although the urban stretch is tarmac or gravelled, some of the rural stretches may be wet or muddy.
- Walk only in daylight – towpaths are rarely lighted.
- Bring sufficient food supplies and stay hydrated.
- Be aware of the dangers of being in close proximity to water, particularly around lock chambers, and also be aware of the dangers of walking on public road sections.
- Tell someone where you are walking and carry a mobile phone.
- Don't overdo it!
- Be aware that there may be occasions when construction and maintenance works being carried out on the canal can affect access.

Suggested Walking Routes

1) Urban Royal Canal – Newcomen Bridge to Ashtown

This is a 6 km urban walkway, following the route of the canal from the 1st Lock at Newcomen Bridge to the 10th Lock at Ashtown. You could avail of the option to follow the route to 10th Lock and then catch a train back into the city at Ashtown Station.

2) Royal Canal – Ashtown to Mullingar

This is a 77 km, long-distance walking trail stretching from the 10th Lock at Ashtown to Mullingar. The suggested sections numbered 1 – 7 divide this length into half day walking routes. Refer also to the relevant maps from page 32 onwards.

3) Royal Canal – Mullingar to the Shannon

Although most of this section is not currently waymarked, the 61 km of the Royal Canal beyond Mullingar and westward to the Shannon is walkable. The suggested sections numbered 8 – 14 divide this length into manageable walking routes. Refer also to the relevant maps from page 48 onwards.

Section	Route	Map Ref	Terrain	KM
1	Ashtown (10th Lock) to Cope Bridge	Maps 1b/2	About 9 km grassy bank, 2.5 km path/track. After leaving the station it can be wet; path is high above the canal through "The Deep Sinking". Good walking surface mainly. Cross the canal at Kennan Bridge.	11.5
2	Cope Bridge, Lexlip Confey Station to Maynooth Harbour	Maps 2/3	About 4 km grassy bank, 3.5 km track. All on north side of canal.	7.5
3	Maynooth Harbour to McLoughlin Bridge (17th Lock) Fern's Lock	Maps 3/4	About 0.5 km track, remainder grassy track. All on north side of canal.	9.75
4	McLoughlin Bridge (17th Lock) Fern's Lock to Enfield Bridge	Maps 4/5	About 1 km road, 2 km track, 6 km grassy track.	9
5	Enfield Bridge to Hill of Down	Maps 5/6	About 5.75 km track/unsealed road, 9.25 km grassy bank.	15
6	Hill of Down to Riverstown Bridge	Maps 6/7	About 4 km road, 6.25 km track/ unsealed road.	10.25
7	Riverstown Bridge to Mullingar (Moran's Bridge)	Maps 8/9	About 2 km road, 3.5 km unsealed road/ track, 8.5 km grassy bank.	14
8	Mullingar (Moran's Bridge) to Ballinea Bridges	Map 9	Tarmac footpath/cyclepath to Ballinea Bridge. About 6.5 km on the south bank to Belmont Bridge, then cross to north bank for 0.5 km to Ballinea Bridge	7
9	Ballinea Bridges to Ballynacargy Harbour	Maps 10/11	Grass bank on south bank to Kildallan Bridge for 7.5 km, then gravel track 5 km along south bank to Ballynacargy.	12.5
10	Ballynacargy Harbour to Abbeyshrule Harbour	Map 11	Gravel track to Kelly's Bridge for 3 km, then grass bank almost the whole way to Abbeyshrule, 4.75 km, with gravel track for the final km into Abbeyshrule. All on south bank.	8.75
11	Abbeyshrule Harbour to Ballybrannigan Harbour	Map 12	Grass bank on south bank, with short section of gravel track between Draper's Bridge and Allard's Bridge for 1.5 km. North bank also walkable from Allard's Bridge to Ballybrannigan Harbour (grass bank – 3 km; gravel track – 3 km).	9
12	Ballybrannigan Harbour to Coolnahinch Bridge	Maps 12/13	Grass bank on south bank, possibly rough in places.	11
13	Coolnahinch Bridge to Ballinamore or Lyneen Bridge	Map 13	All on Road.	3
14	Ballinamore or Lyneen Bridge to Richmond Harbour, Cloondara	Maps 13/14	About 3.25 km of grass bank on south bank to Aghnaskea Bridge, Kilashee; then gravel track to Cloondara for 6.25 km.	9.5

Further reading

Irish Waterside Walks, Michael Fewer, 1997. Gill and Macmillan.
Visit **www.walkireland.ie**

CYCLING ON THE ROYAL CANAL

Introduction

The National Cycle Network has recently identified a number of cycle hub towns across the country. Several looped cycle routes have been developed in each hub town, consisting of half day and day cycles. One of the hub towns is Mullingar, where the designated routes along quiet country roads are enriched by the town's proximity to several beautiful waterways; Mullingar is skirted by the Royal Canal (Map 9), nestles beside Lough Ennell and is linked to Lough Owel via the Lough Owel Feeder (Map 16). Mullingar itself is a busy market town with excellent facilities and amenities.

It should be noted that canal towpaths in general are not suitable for cycling due to their surfacing and the potential for damage to be caused to the natural environment. However, the towpath of the Royal Canal between Mullingar and Ballinea (which runs along the south bank to Belmont Bridge and then on the north bank to Ballinea Bridge) has been specifically upgraded to ensure the safety of all users of the towpath section of the cycle route. Waterways Ireland will continue to participate in discussions regarding the Government's sustainable *"Smarter Travel"* transport policy and in particular the *"National Cycle Policy Framework 2009 – 2020"* as it relates to the canal.

Looped Cycle Routes

Interpretation Boards have been erected at strategic locations along the cycle routes. There are 3 routes to choose from around Mullingar:-

Loop 1: North of Mullingar around Lough Owel

Distance: 30 kilometres   **Time**: 2-3 hours

Start out at Mullingar Railway Station travelling north. Take a break at Portnashangan and take in the view of Lough Owel and Church Island. Continue north to the village of Multyfarnham. Follow the route back on the western side of the lake.

Loop 2: Tour of the countryside between Lough Owel and Lough Ennell

Distance: 49 kilometres   **Time**: 4-5 hours

Start by following Loop 1 in reverse until you pass the high point of Frewin Hill. The route then takes a southerly direction along quiet roads and lanes, crossing the occasional main road. A good place to stop is at the pretty Coolnahay Harbour on the Royal Canal. Continue on to Castletown Geoghegan, the route then takes you to scenic Lilliput at Lough Ennell. Return is via Loop 3 to Ballinea, with the final stretch along the Royal Canal towpath.

Loop 3: South of Mullingar to Lilliput and around Lough Ennell

Distance: 38 kilometres   **Time**: 3-4 hours

Start again at Mullingar Railway Station, travelling south along the Royal
Canal towpath towards Lilliput, a beautiful amenity area with stunning views
of Lough Ennell. Lilliput is the inspiration for the enchanting tale – Gulliver's
Travels. Travelling via Dalystown & Gaybrook on the eastern side of Lough
Ennell, continue on towards the lakeshore again with a visit to Belvedere
House, Gardens and Park.

Further information

For further details visit **www.discoverireland.ie/westmeath**

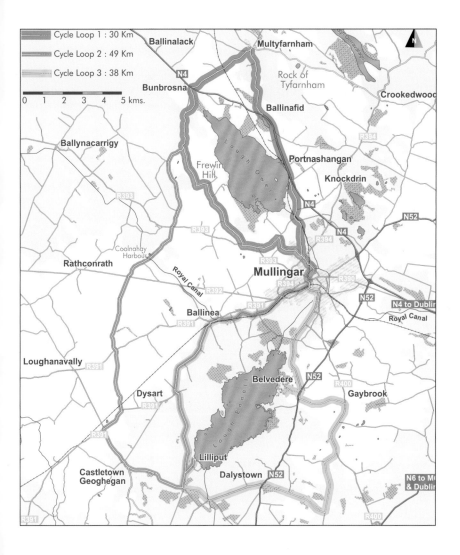

CANOEING THE ROYAL CANAL

Canoeing is the collective term used to describe a wide-ranging and multi-faceted activity that encompasses competitive and non-competitive forms of canoeing and kayaking. In non–sport related canoeing the generic term "canoeing" is used to describe the less formalised types of kayaking and canoeing activities that are mainly based on journeying and adventuring.

Within sport related canoeing there are opportunities to take part in numerous specialised competitive canoeing disciplines such as canoe slalom, marathon racing, flat water racing, freestyle, and canoe polo.

One of the best ways to get to know what canoeing has to offer you is to join a local group/club or alternatively undertake one of the Canoe Union's training courses – it's more fun, safer and will help you master basic skills more quickly. Under expert guidance you will learn basic techniques, and the simple safety rules that will equip you to enjoy a lifetime of water activities.

The Royal Canal is tailor-made for both recreational and competitive canoeing – offering simple touring on placid water or excellent location for competitive disciplines such as flat water racing or for canoe polo. There are a number of canoe clubs based on the Royal Canal such as Kilcock Canoe Polo Club (which hosted the European Canoe Polo Championship in 2006), North Kildare Canoe Club, Royal Canal Canoe Club in Killucan, Inny Kayak Club in Ballymahon and Mullingar Canoe Club. Further details can be found on **www.canoe.ie**

Kayaking

Kayaking as a recreational activity provides opportunities for adventure, relaxation, exploration and competition. The challenge of descending a white-water river, or gracefully meandering quiet lakes and canals are both part of canoeing's special appeal. Kayaks are frequently used for expeditions at sea and represent the ideal craft for close investigation of Ireland's spectacular coastlines. Kayaking has long been recognised as a useful medium for outdoor education, and is of particular value in building confidence, self-reliance and co-operation.

Kayaks now come in many different forms but whatever their shape and appearance, the feature which identifies a craft as a kayak is that the occupant or occupants sit and use a double bladed paddle.

Canoeing

Many indigenous peoples have developed "canoe" crafts. The modern "Canadian Canoe" derives from a canoe form evolved by the native North American Indians, who used native birch bark to fashion a light, versatile craft.

Modern "open canoes", now used mainly for recreational touring, employ modern materials, but their shape remains virtually unchanged from the age-old designs of their ancestors.

The open canoe is a relatively stable and immensely versatile craft which is normally paddled by two people but can be handled solo. To learn to paddle a canoe as a doubles pair requires effective communication and the development of good teamwork between partners. It is perhaps these characteristics which represent part of its worth as an educational medium, but it is the unique potential of the canoe as a "journeying craft" that is responsible for its rapidly heightening profile both in education and recreation.

Other forms of canoes have been developed, mainly for specialised use in competition; but regardless of shape, a craft is identified as a canoe if the occupant or occupants would normally kneel and use a single bladed paddle.

Safety

As a water-based activity/sport, canoeing has an inescapable element of inherent risk. The answer to managing this risk lies in a combination of training based on the accepted code of technique and safety, and experience gathered over a number of years, where techniques are acquired and practiced. For detailed safety guidelines and environmental considerations, you should visit **www.canoe.ie**

WILDLIFE ON THE ROYAL CANAL

Canals are man-made linear networks of navigable waterway which traverse the countryside. During their heyday in the early 1800s, the wildlife of the system remained constant as it was influenced by boat traffic on the canals and user pressure on the towpath. When trading on the Royal Canal ceased in the 1950s, it soon developed into a semi-natural wildlife park.

Along the western sections the towpath became overgrown with Bramble which, over time, was replaced by mixed scrub. Scrub also developed along the channel bed. The scrub was of two distinct types: on the dry towpath habitat species such as Hazel, Hawthorn, Blackthorn, Guelder-rose and Spindle grew; while in the channel edge those species favouring wetter conditions such as Willow and Alder grew.

With the restoration of the Royal Canal as a navigable waterway, some of the scrub habitat has been lost. However this has provided an opportunity for other habitats, which had existed when the canal was first built and which had since been choked out by the scrub, to develop.

Deep Waterway

Milfoils and Pondweeds grow in the deeper water. A range of tiny invertebrates such as snails and insect larvae thrive on these plants. These form the food supply for the many coarse fish found in the canal. Swans and ducks feed on the Yellow Water-lily and tiny Duckweeds which float on the surface.

Reed Fringe

The reed fringe grows in shallower water at the edge of the canal. It is dominated by reeds and sedges interspersed with such other plants as Bogbean, Greater and Lesser Spearwort and Marsh Marigold. The reed fringe acts as a buffer which disperses wave energy, caused by wind and boats, and so prevents bank erosion. It helps to maintain the health of the waterway as the growing plants use up excess nutrients which otherwise might encourage algal growth. It also provides food and shelter for waterfowl such as the Moorhen; fish such as Pike and a range of aquatic invertebrates. Damselflies and dragonflies hover about above the reed fringe. The larvae spend the early part of their lives under water and crawl up the emergent plant to shed their skin and fly away as adults.

Bank

The canal bank which lies between the channel and the towpath is a transitional zone between land and water. Here, early in the year the Yellow Iris and Cuckooflower are found. Caterpillars of the aptly-named Orange-tip Butterfly feed on the Cuckooflower. Other plants on the bank are Marsh Orchids, Common Valerian, the heavily scented cream-coloured Meadowsweet, and Hemp Agrimony. Many Red Admiral and Small Tortoiseshell butterflies feed on the Hemp Agrimony.

Grassland

There is a selection of grassland types to be found along the Royal Canal. Controlled grazing is carried out along some stretches. With this approach the vigorous species such as Nettles, Hogweeds and Docks do not get a chance to dominate. Instead, less competitive plants such as Cowslips, Orchids and many more grow, resulting in a wide diversity. Allowing a meadow to develop is another option which again favours ecological diversity. In this instance, the less competitive species have a chance to grow and set seed before they are cut. The advantages of hay meadows are many from the wildlife point of view: the diversity of the seed-bank is maintained; plants once common in the countryside but now on the decline as a result of modern farming techniques thrive along the canal grasslands; insects can develop and feed off their favoured host plants; these in turn become a food source for birds and other small mammals.

Boundary Hedgerows

For most of its length the Royal Canal, especially on the towpath side, has a hedgerow with Hawthorn predominating. On the non-towpath side most of the scrub which grew when the canal was closed to navigation has been allowed to remain. The hedgerow and scrub provide a valuable habitat for wildlife. Birds and small mammals are attracted to the area as there is a plentiful supply of fruit and berries for the herbivores and insects for the carnivores and omnivores. Hawthorn alone supports over a hundred insect species. The butterflies and moths and their caterpillars are the most conspicious inverte-brates. Larger mammals such as Otters also take cover in the dense scrub at the water's edge. Spring is the best time to see the flowers of the hedge. The white blooms of the Blackthorn appear before the leaves. These are followed by the white flowers of the Hawthorn and Elder. The ground layer plants including Primroses and Celandines also flower in Spring.

Stonework

In the past the stone bridges and locks had become overgrown with Ivy and Sycamore which choked out typical wall plants. With restoration wall plants such as the Rustyback, Wall-rue, Hart's-tongue and Maidenhair Spleenwort ferns and the tiny White Stonecrop can now be seen.

Conservation

As well as maximising the navigational potential of the canal, Waterways Ireland is also committed to maximising its amenity potential, catering for the needs of anglers, walkers and wildlife enthusiasts. To this end, the restoration of the Royal Canal has been carried out in a sensitive and balanced manner, taking full account of the canal's importance as an environmental resource.

Photographs courtesy of the National Biodiversity Data Centre.

Further reading

Nature on Irish Canals, produced by Dúchas, the Heritage Service. Provides more detailed information on the flora and fauna along canals. Available from Waterways Ireland at a cost of €4.40 Visit **www.waterwaysireland.org**

ATTRACTIONS ALONG THE ROYAL CANAL

Within a short distance of the Royal Canal, there are many attractions, ranging from architectural to arts and crafts, leisure to sports, entertainment to relaxation. What follows is not intended as comprehensive travel guide, but it will give a flavour of the diversity and quality of those attractions which are most easily accessible from the Royal Canal. You should make contact by telephone, or access the relevant website for further information including opening times.

Urban Dublin itself is compact, ideal for exploring on foot. This first section gives details of the attractions that are in closest proximity to the canal as it passes through this cosmopolitan and colourful city.

For details about other attractions, you should contact Dublin Tourism on +353 (0)1 605 7700 or **www.visitdublin.com**

Dublin Zoo, Phoenix Park Dublin 8
Website: www.dublinzoo.ie
Contact +353 (0)1 474 8900
Located in Phoenix Park, Dublin, this is the largest zoo in Ireland and one of Dublin's most popular attractions. Opened in 1831, the zoo's role today is that of conservation, study, and education. Covering over 24 hectares of Phoenix Park, it provides a habitat for more than 235 species of wild animals and tropical birds. The zoo is divided into areas named World of Cats, World of Primates, Fringes of the Arctic, African Plains, Birds, Reptiles, Plants, City Farm and Endangered Species.

Phoenix Park, Visitors Centre and Ashtown Castle,
Phoenix Park, Dublin 8
Website: www.phoenixpark.ie
Contact +353 (0)1 677 0095
The Phoenix Park at 707 hectares is one of the largest enclosed recreational spaces within any European capital city. It was established in 1662 originally as a Royal deer park. About 30% of the Phoenix Park is covered by trees and is a sanctuary for many mammals and birds.
Ashtown Demesne, accessed off the Phoenix roundabout on Chesterfield Avenue, has numerous attractions for young and old alike.They include Ashtown Castle, a Victorian Kitchen Walled Garden, Phoenix Park Visitor Centre, Phoenix Cafe, toilets, car and coach parking, woodland walks, picnic area and new universal access playground. The Phoenix Park Visitor Centre has a historical interpretation and an audio-visual presentation of the Phoenix Park throughout the ages. The park is also home to the oldest cricket club in Ireland, founded in 1830.
Áras an Uachtaráin, the residence of the President of Ireland dates from 1750 and is located in the centre of the park adjacent to the United States Ambassador's residence, which was built in 1774.

Croke Park and GAA Museum, North Dublin between Drumcondra
and Ballybough
Website: www.crokepark.ie
Contact + 353 (0)1 819 2300
The home of Gaelic Games, headquarters of the GAA (Gaelic Athletic
Association), and with a capacity for 82,300 people, Croke Park has been
at the heart of Irish sporting life for over a hundred years. With a prime
location in central Dublin and a tradition that is steeped in history, Croke Park
stadium is an inspirational venue not only for GAA supporters and players
but also for spectacular performances and other sporting events which have
included:- Muhammad Ali fought here in 1972; concerts from U2, Robbie
Williams, The Police, Neil Diamond, Westlife, Tina Turner and Bon Jovi;
the opening and closing ceremonies of the 2003 Special Olympics World
Summer Games; International rugby and soccer fixtures.
The GAA Museum, situated under the Cusack Stand in Croke Park, was
established to commemorate, recognise and celebrate the GAA's enormous
contribution to Irish sporting, cultural and social life since its foundation
in 1884.

Rural Royal – as the canal wends its way westwards, there are numerous attractions which will enhance the experience of a visit to the waterway. You should make contact by telephone, or access the relevant website for further information, including opening times. For details about other attractions, visit the Discover Ireland website at www.discoverireland.ie

Castletown House, Celbridge, Co.Kildare
Website: www.castletown.ie
Contact +353 (0)1 628 8252
Castletown is Ireland's largest and earliest Palladian style house and was built between 1722 and 1729 for William Conolly, Speaker of the Irish House of Commons and the wealthiest commoner in Ireland. The property is now managed by the Office of Public Works. Through restoration, conservation, acquisition of parkland and development of visitor facilities, their long term objective is to preserve for future generations one of the most important houses in Ireland and one of significance in terms of European architectural heritage.

Carton House, Maynooth, Co.Kildare
Website: www.cartonhouse.com
Contact +353 (0)1 505 2000
Once the home of the Duke of Leinster, Carton House has been remodelled as a luxury hotel, spa and golf course.

Maynooth Castle, Maynooth Village, Co.Kildare
Website: www.maynoothcastle@opw.ie
Contact +353 (0)1 628 6744
This great stone castle was founded in the early 13th century. The original keep, constructed c. 1203, was one of the largest of its kind in Ireland. Early in the 17th century the castle was remodelled and the main focus of the castle shifted from the original keep to the buildings in the east of the grounds. It was vested in the State in 1991 and a programme of restoration commenced in February 2000. There is an exhibition in the keep on the history of the castle and the family.

Larchill Arcadian Gardens, Larchill, Kilcock
Website: www.larchill.ie
Contact +353 (0)1 628 7354
The gardens are **open during the summer season only** – contact before visiting for opening times or check website. Larchill was created originally in the mid 18th century as a 'Ferme Ornée' (Ornamental Farm) and, having been rediscovered, is the only surviving complete garden of its type in Europe. Scenic walks through parkland and beech avenues link 10 magical garden follies. Rare breeds of cattle and sheep graze the land. There is a picturesque lake with two fairytale island follies, a formal walled garden with shell lined tower and a decorative gothic farmyard.

Clonard Heritage Trail, Clonard, Co.Meath
Website: www.meath.ie/tourism/heritage/heritagetrails/clonardheritagetrail
Contact +353 (0)46 909 7060
The ancient name for this place was Ross Finnchuil. Later in the Irish speaking days it was known as Cluain Ioraird, or the meadow of Ioraird, Ioraird believed to be a local landlord. Now it is known as Clonard, a place made famous by the monastic school of St Finian in the 6th century. The trail takes in the eponymous Church, Statue and Well, together with several other sites of heritage significance.

Mullingar Arts Centre, Mount Street, Mullingar
Website: www.mulllingarartscentre.ie
Contact +353 (0)44 93 47777
Mullingar Arts Centre opened its doors to the public on 1st January 1999. The Arts Centre is contained in the totally re-furbished County Hall and comprises a 407 seat theatre, two art workshops and an exquisitely lit art gallery. The workshops cater for all art forms. The centre offers courses for children and adults in arts, piano, Irish dancing and ballet. Theatre events include drama, concerts, recitals, opera and children's shows.

Belvedere House, Gardens and Park, Belvedere, Tullamore Road, Mullingar, Co.Westmeath
Website: www.belvedere-house.ie
Contact +353 (0)44 934 9060
The Estate comprises 65 hectares of parkland with 6 km of magnificent woodland and lakeshore walks, including the Narnia Trail. Several follies adorn the landscape including Ireland's largest folly, The Jealous Wall. The restored Belvedere House is an 18th Century hunting/fishing lodge designed by the renowned German architect Richard Castle for Robert Rochfort, later the 1st Earl of Belvedere. A fascinating walled garden, designed by Ninian Nevin in 1857, contains one of Ireland's finest collections of rare and special plants. The stable block is home to a modern visitor centre with multi-media show, exhibitions and fully licensed cafe. Adjacent to the visitor centre are two children's play areas. There is also a delightful tram, which provides guided tours around a section of the parkland on selected days throughout the year. Belvedere is open year round with a full calendar of events.
A visit to Belvedere forms part of the recommended Loop 3 cycle route – see previous section "Cycling on the Royal Canal".

Ledwithstown House, Co.Longford
Contact + 353 (0)90 643 2382 (**Open to visitors by appointment only**).
One and a half kilometres south of Foigha Bridge is Ledwithstown House, a very interesting small Georgian house built in 1746, the design of which is attributed to Richard Cassels. Originally the seat of the Ledwith family, the estate at one time covered some 800 hectares. The last of the family to live there, William Ledwith, left in 1891. In 1911 the property was bought by Laurence Feeney, grandfather of the present owner. The house is at present being painstakingly restored and is open to visitors by appointment.

Corlea Trackway Visitor Centre, Keenagh, Co. Longford
Website: www.heritageireland.ie/en/midlandseastcoast/
corleayrackwayvisitorcentre/
Contact +353 (0)43 332 2386 (**Open April to September only**).
The centre interprets an Iron Age bog road that was built in the year 148
B.C. across the boglands of Longford, close to the River Shannon. The oak
road is the largest of its kind to have been uncovered in Europe and was
excavated by Professor Barry Raftery of University College Dublin. Inside
the interpretative centre, an 18 m stretch of the preserved trackway is
on permanent display in a hall specially designed to preserve the ancient
wooden structure. Bord na Móna and the Office of Public Works have carried
out conservation work on the surrounding bog to ensure that it remains wet
and that the buried road remains preserved.

St Mel's Ecclesiastical Museum, Longford Town, Co. Longford
(Advance booking is required)
St Mel's Diocesan Museum is situated towards the rear of St Mel's Cathedral.
There are many historical and interesting exhibits in St Mel's Museum. A
Crosier believed to have belonged to St Mel was found at Ardagh near the
old cathedral of St Mel and is kept in the Museum. It dates back to the mid
tenth century.

CHRONOLOGICAL HISTORY

1755	Survey made by Thomas Williams and John Cooley for a canal from Dublin to the north Shannon using the rivers Ryewater, Blackwater, Boyne, Deel, Yellow, Lough Derravaragh and the rivers Inny and Camlin.
1756	The more southerly Grand Canal route is chosen by the Commissioners of Inland Navigation.
1789	Aid sought to build a canal from Dublin to Tarmonbarry reviving the old plans. Parliament grants £66,000 to add to the £134,000 promised by subscribers. The charter of the Royal Canal Company enrolled.
1796	Canal opened to Kilcock.
1806	Canal completed to Mullingar.
1807	Royal Canal Hotel at Moyvalley opened.
1809	Canal completed to Coolnahay at the western end of the summit level.
1811-13	Company's debt rises to £862,000 despite government grants and loans amounting to £143,856. Parliamentary investigations into the company's affairs and discussions about the line of the canal to the Shannon.
1813	The Royal Canal Company dissolved and the concern handed over to the Directors General of Inland Navigation with instructions to complete the canal at public expense.
1817	Canal completed to the Shannon at Tarmonbarry. Total cost of the canal from Dublin £1,421,954.
1818	The New Royal Canal Company takes over the canal with a government Board of Control to watch over its affairs.
1830	The Longford Branch is opened.
1830s	Average annual tonnage carried 80,000 tons and 40,000 passengers.

1845	The entire concern is purchased by the Midland Great Western Railway Company for £298,059 with a view to using the property alongside the canal to lay a railway to the west.
1873	Spencer Dock completed.
1877	Broadstone Harbour filled in as forecourt for the railway terminus.
1880s	Average tonnage reduced to 30,000 tons.
1927	Further section of Broadstone Branch filled in. Annual tonnage reduced to 10,000 tons in the 1920s.
1938	Ownership transferred to the Great Southern Railway.
1939-45	Brief revival of trade during the Emergency Years.
1944	Ownership transferred to Córas Iompair Éireann (CIE).
1946	L.T.C. Rolt navigated the canal and recorded his trip in Green & Silver.
1951	Last bye-trader, James Leech of Killucan, ceased to operate.
1955	Douglas Heard's Hark was the last officially recorded boat to pass through the canal, and he made a film of the trip.
1956	The remainder of the Broadstone Branch filled in.
1961	The canal was officially closed to navigation.
1974	The IWAI 'Save the Royal Canal' campaign began and the Royal Canal Amenity Group was formed.
1986	Ownership transferred to The Office of Public Works.
1990	74km re-opened to navigation, 12th Lock to Mullingar.
1996	Ownership transferred to the Department of Arts, Culture and the Gaeltacht.
2000	Ownership transferred to Waterways Ireland.
2000-2009	Replacement by Waterways Ireland of all remaining culverted crossings of the Main Line.
2010	Main Line due to be reopened between Spencer Dock, Dublin and the River Shannon.

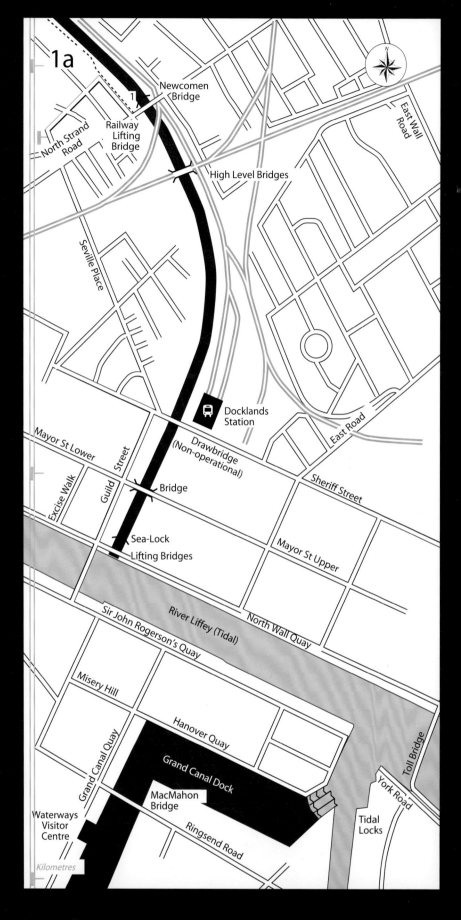

1a

Newcomen Bridge

North Strand Road

Railway Lifting Bridge

High Level Bridges

Seville Place

East Wall Road

Docklands Station

Mayor St Lower

Excise Walk

Guild Street

Drawbridge (Non-operational)

East Road

Sheriff Street

Bridge

Sea-Lock

Lifting Bridges

Mayor St Upper

River Liffey (Tidal)

Sir John Rogerson's Quay

North Wall Quay

Misery Hill

Grand Canal Quay

Hanover Quay

Grand Canal Dock

Toll Bridge

MacMahon Bridge

York Road

Waterways Visitor Centre

Ringsend Road

Tidal Locks

Kilometres

SECTION 1A – SPENCER DOCK (entry to Royal Canal from River Liffey and Grand Canal)

Route Description

The Royal Canal begins at Spencer Dock on the north bank of the tidal River Liffey. Entrance to the dock is under the pair of North Wall lifting bridges and through the sea lock. Spencer Dock was formerly a wide stretch of waterway extending for one kilometre and crossed by Sheriff Street drawbridge (Spencer Bridge) as well as closely-spaced high level bridges carrying railway lines into Connolly Station. In the 1970s, some of the dock area was in-filled and partly built over by CIE, considerably narrowing the canal throughout the length of the dock. All buildings and the infill between the sea lock and Spencer Bridge have now been removed. The remaining infill will be removed as redevelopment of the Spencer Dock area proceeds.

In 2009 a new bridge built above the sea lock re-connected Upper and Lower Mayor Street, a connection that was severed in the 1790s when the construction of the Royal Canal commenced. This bridge carries the Luas Red Line C1 to The Point.

At the inner end of Spencer Dock, just below Newcomen Bridge, a single track railway loop line crosses the canal at low level on a lifting bridge. Sheriff Street drawbridge is not at present operational and it is unlikely that it will be brought back into use in the immediate future. Beside the bridge, a 110kV electric cable crosses the dock at towpath level. Both the bridge and cable obstruct the navigation although by judicious management of the water level within the dock it is possible for boats to achieve a passage. Anyone contemplating this journey, either to or from the River Liffey or Grand Canal Basin, should first contact Waterways Ireland Eastern Regional Office at Floor 2 Block C, Ashtowngate, Navan Road, Dublin 15. Tel: +353 (0)1 868 0148.

Facilities/Services

Pub & restaurants: North Wall Quay.
Pubs, restaurants, shops: Mayor Street Lower, Excise Walk.
Railway Stations: Docklands, Connolly.

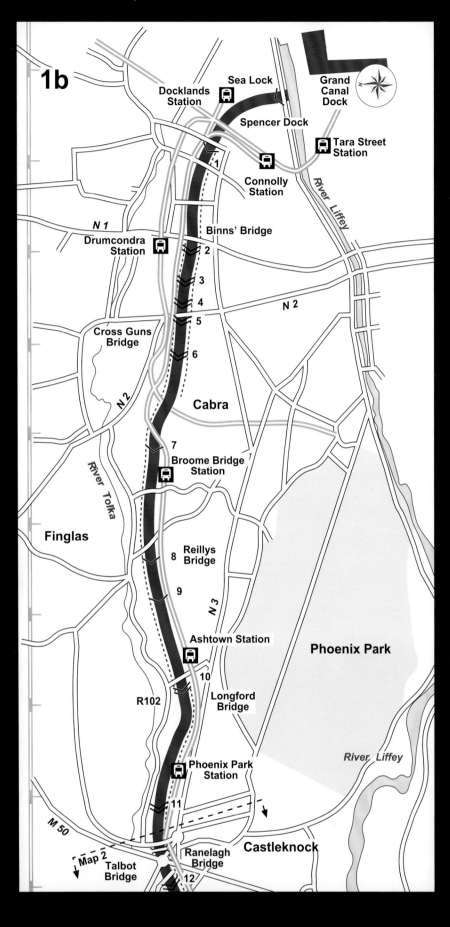

1b

Docklands Station

Sea Lock

Grand Canal Dock

Spencer Dock

Tara Street Station

1

Connolly Station

River Liffey

N 1

Drumcondra Station

Binns' Bridge

2

3

4

N 2

5

Cross Guns Bridge

6

N 2

Cabra

7

Broome Bridge Station

River Tolka

Finglas

8

Reillys Bridge

9

N 3

Ashtown Station

Phoenix Park

10

Longford Bridge

R102

Phoenix Park Station

River Liffey

11

M 50

Castleknock

Map 2

Talbot Bridge

Ranelagh Bridge

12

SECTION 1B – SPENCER DOCK, DUBLIN TO 12TH LOCK, BLANCHARDSTOWN

Route Description

Beyond the 1st Lock the canal rises steeply out of the city through a succession of double locks passing Croke Park, Mountjoy Prison, and the junction with the former Broadstone Branch of the canal, which is now filled in. Just below the 7th Lock, at Liffey Junction, the railway line to the west crosses the canal to the south side along which it is to be a constant companion all the way to Ballinea Bridge, west of Mullingar. From Longford Bridge the canal tends to leave the city behind and begins to assume a more rural aspect which continues for almost the whole of its remaining 138 km to the River Shannon. There is a very attractive tree-lined stretch of waterway between the 10th and 11th Locks, but it is soon followed by the complex of bridges and an aqueduct associated with the junction of the M50 motorway and the Navan Road (N3).

Facilities

Pubs, shops: Binns' Bridge & Cross Guns Bridge.
Café, shops: Ashtown (Longford Bridge).
Pub: Ashtown (Navan Road 400 m).
Hotel: Talbot Bridge.
Railway Stations: Drumcondra, Broome Bridge & Ashtown. (Note: although situated alongside the towpath, there is no access to the canal from Phoenix Park station).
Bus Services: Ashtown (station) 120. Ashtown (Navan Road 400 m) 37, 38, 38a, 38b, 38c, 39, 39a, 39b, 39c, 70, 70a. Talbot Bridge (Navan Road, Blanchardstown 500 m) 38, 38a, 38c, 39, 39a, 39c, 70, 70a, 237.

History

Work began on the Dublin sections of the Royal Canal in 1789 and continued through the 1790s with many delays caused by inaccurate surveys. The Broadstone Branch was not completed until 1801. Foster Aqueduct, a well-known city landmark on this branch, was demolished in 1951. There was a hotel at Broadstone Harbour, part of which became No. 1 Phibsborough Road. Drinking water was drawn from the harbour for the nearby City Basin until the 1860s. The Royal Canal Company reneged on its obligation to build docks at the junction with the River Liffey. Spencer Dock, which opened in 1873, was eventually constructed by the Midland Great Western Railway Company which had bought the canal in 1845. Hamilton Bridge (formerly Broome Bridge) is notable for its connection with the Dublin-born mathematician and Astronomer Royal, Sir William Rowan Hamilton. In 1958 Dublin Corporation approved the renaming of the bridge in honour of Sir William Rowan Hamilton, but the original name is still often used.

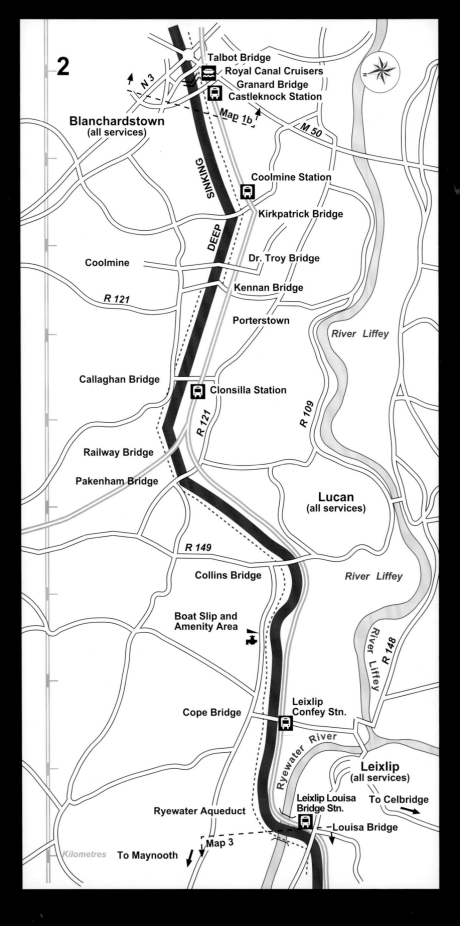

2

↗ N 3

Talbot Bridge
Royal Canal Cruisers
Granard Bridge
Castleknock Station

Blanchardstown
(all services)

Map 1b

M 50

SINKING

DEEP

Coolmine Station

Kirkpatrick Bridge

Coolmine

Dr. Troy Bridge

Kennan Bridge

R 121

Porterstown

River Liffey

Callaghan Bridge

Clonsilla Station

R 121

R 109

Railway Bridge

Pakenham Bridge

Lucan
(all services)

R 149

Collins Bridge

River Liffey

Boat Slip and
Amenity Area

River Liffey

R 148

Cope Bridge

Leixlip
Confey Stn.

Ryewater River

Leixlip
(all services)

Leixlip Louisa
Bridge Stn.

To Celbridge →

Ryewater Aqueduct

Louisa Bridge

Kilometres

To Maynooth

Map 3

SECTION 2 – BLANCHARDSTOWN TO LOUISA BRIDGE, NEAR LEIXLIP

Route Description

Leaving 12th Lock, Blanchardstown, the canal soon enters the Deep Sinking. At its deepest the towpath is carried some 9 m above the water. Care should be taken when passing through this stretch as the channel width is very restricted. Beyond the cutting the canal passes under a new bridge that from 2010 will carry the reopened line of the Dublin & Meath Railway. There is a good road approach to the boat slipway near Leixlip which gives access to this 12 km long level. Soon, the canal bends sharply to the south and canal and railway are carried across the Ryewater by a massive earth embankment with the river flowing through a tunnel 30 m below. Overlooking the aqueduct is the derelict house of the lengthsman, once responsible for this stretch of canal. Between the aqueduct and Louisa Bridge and just west of the canal are the remains of Leixlip Spa, which was discovered by workmen building the embankment in the 1790s and became a fashionable watering place.

Facilities

All Services: Lucan and Leixlip, some distance south of the canal.
Railway Stations: Castleknock, Coolmine, Clonsilla, Leixlip Confey, Leixlip Louisa Bridge.
Bus Services: Granard Bridge 37, 38b, 237. Kirkpatrick Bridge 237, 239. Callaghan Bridge 39, 239, 439a. Cope Bridge (Captains Hill, 500 m) 66a. Louisa Bridge 66.
Slipway: Confey, between Collins Bridge and Cope Bridge on north bank (Waterways Ireland assistance required – contact the Eastern Regional Office at Floor 2 Block C, Ashtowngate, Navan Road, Dublin 15. Tel: +353 (0)1 868 0148.
Water: Confey Amenity Area (Waterways Ireland assistance required).
Boat Hire: Royal Canal Cruisers, 12th Lock.
Pump-out: Above 12th Lock (Waterways Ireland assistance required).

History

This was a most controversial stretch of the canal because it became generally known that an unnecessary deviation to the south had been made to bring the canal through Maynooth at the request of the Duke of Leinster, who was a prominent member of the company. A more northerly route would have avoided the Deep Sinking and the costly Ryewater Aqueduct. The cutting, hewn and blasted through the hard black calcareous stone, cost more than £40,000, £10,000 of which was spent on tools and gunpowder. The aqueduct took six years to construct and cost £27,000. The Deep Sinking, being so narrow, made the passing of canal boats impossible and the horses towing the boats were sometimes dragged into the canal. In 1845 there was a serious accident in the cutting when the evening passenger boat to Longford from Dublin struck a stone on the side of the canal, heeled over and filled, drowning sixteen people.

The 12 km long level above the 12th Lock was the first restoration project to be tackled by the newly formed Royal Canal Amenity Group (RCAG) in 1974.

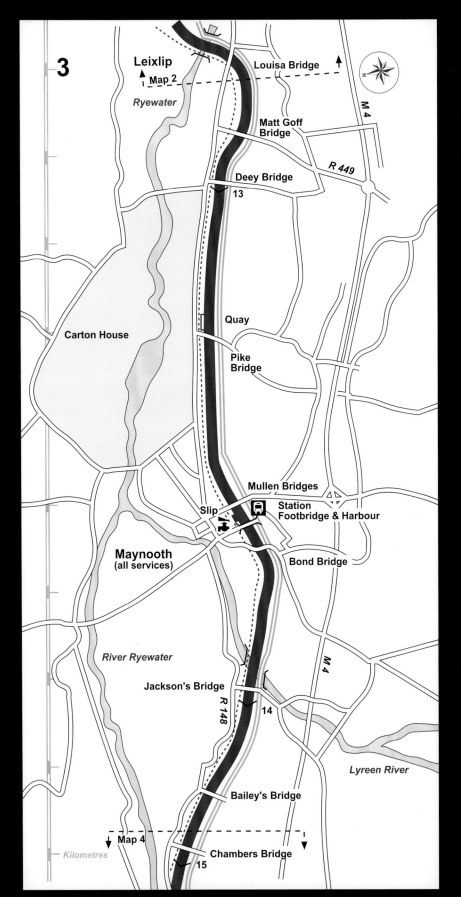

3

Leixlip
↑ Map 2

Ryewater

Louisa Bridge

M 4

Matt Goff
Bridge

R 449

Deey Bridge
13

Carton House

Quay

Pike
Bridge

Mullen Bridges

Slip

Station
Footbridge & Harbour

Maynooth
(all services)

Bond Bridge

River Ryewater

M 4

Jackson's Bridge

R 148

14

Lyreen River

Bailey's Bridge

Map 4

Kilometres

Chambers Bridge
15

SECTION 3 – LOUISA BRIDGE, NEAR LEIXLIP, TO CHAMBER'S BRIDGE, 15TH LOCK, NEAR KILCOCK

Route Description

About 1.5 km from Louisa Bridge, 13th Lock marks the end of the 12 km level from Blanchardstown. The canal is closely hemmed in for the next few kilometres by the road on the north side and the ever present railway on the south bank. The canal skirts the grounds of Carton House, formerly the seat of the Dukes of Leinster, and there is a wharf, or landing place, just east of Pike Bridge which served the Estate. The new Mullen Bridge carrying the Straffan Road across the canal is an excellent example of the combination of modern engineering techniques and a design in complete sympathy with the 200 year old Mullen Bridge alongside. At Maynooth there is a fine harbour and boat slipway. The canal follows the boundary wall of St. Patrick's College before climbing up through two single locks to the 15th level approaching Kilcock. Jackson Bridge at 14th Lock is one of only two bridges on the canal with a separate arch for the towpath, the other being Newcomen Bridge over the tail of the 1st Lock.

Facilities

All Services: Maynooth.
Railway Station: Maynooth.
Bus Services: Maynooth, Dublin Bus services 66, 66X, 67A & Bus Éireann services, 20, 21, 22, 23, 115, 116. R148 road adjoining canal, Dublin Bus service 66.
Slipway: Maynooth Harbour, north bank opposite station (Waterways Ireland assistance required – contact the Eastern Regional Office at Floor 2 Block C, Ashtowngate, Navan Road, Dublin 15. Tel: +353 (0)1 868 0148).
Water: Maynooth Harbour.

History

13th Lock, Deey Bridge, had the reputation among the old Royal Canal boatmen of being haunted and they would never moor there for the night. It was at Carton House that the Duke of Leinster lived who had insisted on the deviation of the canal. The original Carton House was remodelled by Richard Cassels in 1739/47 for the 19th Earl of Kildare in splendid style. After surmounting great difficulties the canal was eventually opened to Kilcock in 1796. Maynooth Harbour, although laid out at this time, was not actually completed until some years later.

St. Patrick's College, Maynooth was established in 1795 *"for the better education of persons professing the Popish or Roman Catholic religion"*, to educate young men at home rather than force them to go to Europe. The buildings are two squares of courts built around the original Stoyte House and the architecture has been the subject of much criticism. At the gateway to the college are the keep, gate-house and the ruins of a Norman Fitzgerald castle; the former Fitzgerald chapel inside the grounds of the college is now the Church of Ireland church.

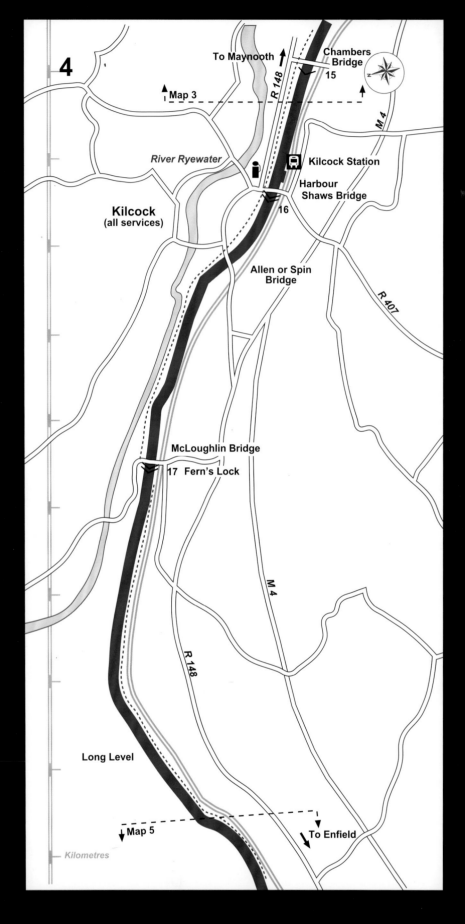

4

To Maynooth

Chambers Bridge
15

R 148

M 4

River Ryewater

Kilcock Station

Harbour
Shaws Bridge
16

Kilcock
(all services)

Allen or Spin
Bridge

R 407

McLoughlin Bridge
17 Fern's Lock

M 4

R 148

Long Level

↑ Map 3

↓ Map 5

To Enfield

Kilometres

SECTION 4 – CHAMBER'S BRIDGE 15TH LOCK, THROUGH KILCOCK

Route Description

Leaving 15th Lock the canal and the road come together again as they approach Kilcock, where it opens out into a fine harbour. Shaw's Bridge and 16th Lock (double) are immediately above the harbour. Then, skirting the town which is almost hidden from view by trees, the canal passes through a most attractive stretch to Allen Bridge, known locally as Spin Bridge. From here is a stretch of 2.5 km to 17th Lock, Fern's or Ferran's Lock (double), the start of the 32 km Long Level to Thomastown. Immediately below 17th Lock an important feeder enters the canal drawn from the upper reaches of the Ryewater which accompanies the canal here for some distance. From 17th Lock to Cloncurry Bridge is an attractive tree-lined stretch of waterway. Following restoration, the towpath is now located on the south bank.

Facilities

All Services: Kilcock.
Railway Station: Kilcock.
Bus Services: Kilcock, Dublin Bus service 66 & Bus Éireann services 19, 115, 116, 117. R148 road adjoining canal, Dublin Bus service 66.
Fuel: Petrol & diesel at garage on R148 road alongside canal close to Kilcock harbour.

History

With the canal completed to Kilcock and some boats in operation by 1796, the company had to seek further aid from parliament to continue the works. This aid was granted reluctantly in the form of a debenture loan of £25,000 because it was felt that this was the only way to safeguard the interests of the many small shareholders who had invested in the company. The company in turn had to agree to complete the canal to the end of the Long Level at Thomastown without seeking further aid.

The stretch from Fern's Lock to Enfield passes through Cappagh Bog and proved a laborious and expensive undertaking with problems caused by the sides slipping and the bottom swelling up. By 1800 the company was once again in financial difficulty and the works were halted just beyond Enfield.

The Kilcock Branch of the RCAG was formed in 1982. Marvellous work was done in the ensuing months and in less than a year the appearance of the canal through Kilcock was transformed. Situated beside a main road, Kilcock Harbour inevitably became the group's showpiece. The opening of the new bypass has restored some peace and calm to the town and added enormously to the amenity potential of the harbour area, particularly in relation to canoeing and canoe polo activities. See also the section "Canoeing the Royal Canal" for further details.

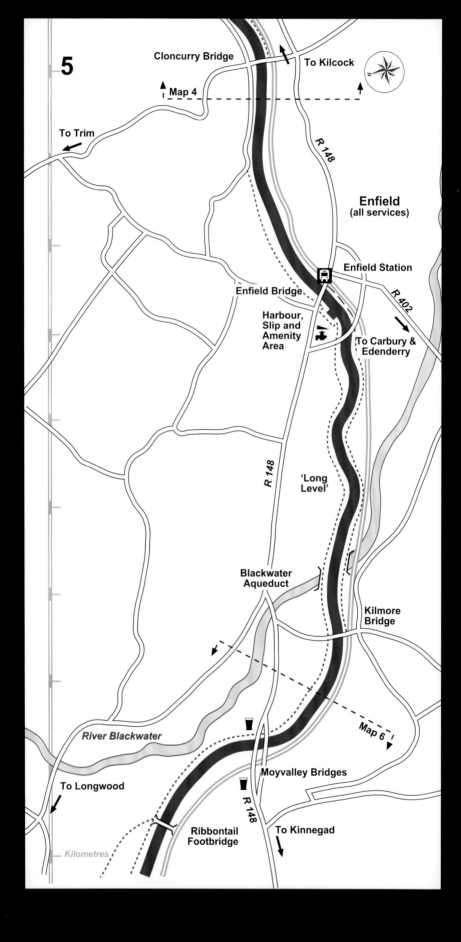

5

Cloncurry Bridge

To Kilcock

Map 4

To Trim

R 148

Enfield
(all services)

Enfield Station

Enfield Bridge

R 402

Harbour,
Slip and
Amenity
Area

To Carbury &
Edenderry

R 148

'Long
Level'

Blackwater
Aqueduct

Kilmore
Bridge

Map 6

River Blackwater

Moyvalley Bridges

To Longwood

R 148

To Kinnegad

Kilometres

Ribbontail
Footbridge

SECTION 5 – CLONCURRY BRIDGE THROUGH ENFIELD TO MOYVALLEY

Route Description

From Cloncurry Bridge the tarred road follows the canal for about 1.5 km before swinging away. Soon the canal enters a deep tree-shaded cutting and passes under the R148 road as it enters Enfield. The harbour is situated on the north bank within the Amenity Park, through which there is access to the slipway. The towpath on the south bank is also surfaced for about 1.5 km with a turning place for cars where it ends. This is a part of the canal much favoured by anglers and frequently used for fishing competitions. Three and a half kilometres beyond Enfield the canal crosses the River Blackwater Aqueduct before reaching Kilmore Bridge. The tree-lined stretch from here to Moyvalley is one of the most attractive on the whole canal.

Facilities

All Services: Enfield.
Pubs & restaurant: Moyvalley.
Railway Station: Enfield.
Bus Services: Enfield, Bus Éireann services 19, 20, 21, 22, 23, 115, 116, 117. Moyvalley (Ballinadrimna Cross), Bus Éireann services 19, 20, 21, 22, 23, 115, 116, 117.
Slipway: Enfield Harbour, north bank.
Water: Enfield Harbour.

History

From Cloncurry Bridge to Enfield the engineers were faced with a difficult section of deep sinking in order to keep the canal on the same level to avoid the need for locks. When the water was eventually admitted, the banks, which were made of fine sand, tended to slip into the canal. The restoration of Enfield Harbour, the construction of the boat slip and the development of the park were all undertaken jointly by the Enfield Community Council and the Enfield Branch of the RCAG, mainly by way of a sponsored Community Youth Training Project and a Social Employment Scheme.

There was once a fine canal hotel at Moyvalley but the ruins were demolished in 1977 to make way for the approach road for a new bridge. The hotel opened to travellers in 1807 and in the years that followed it was reported to be "the best of its kind and the best kept of any in Ireland". Then business began to decline and the canal company sought a tenant but he did not fare much better. In the 1820s when the Ribbonmen (an illegal organisation whose aim was to protect the interests of the working classes) were active in the area and were carrying out attacks on the boats, a local police force was drafted and stationed here. Another attempt to operate a hotel failed in the 1830s and, eventually, the building was purchased by a Mr. Switzer who set up a Hydropathy establishment and built a Bath House. This proved a successful venture for some years but, eventually, Mr. Switzer decided to close down, although he continued to live in the house until his death in 1891. Thereafter, there were a number of owners until the last inhabitant, a Mr. Mulvaney, vacated the house in the 1930s and it gradually became ruinous.

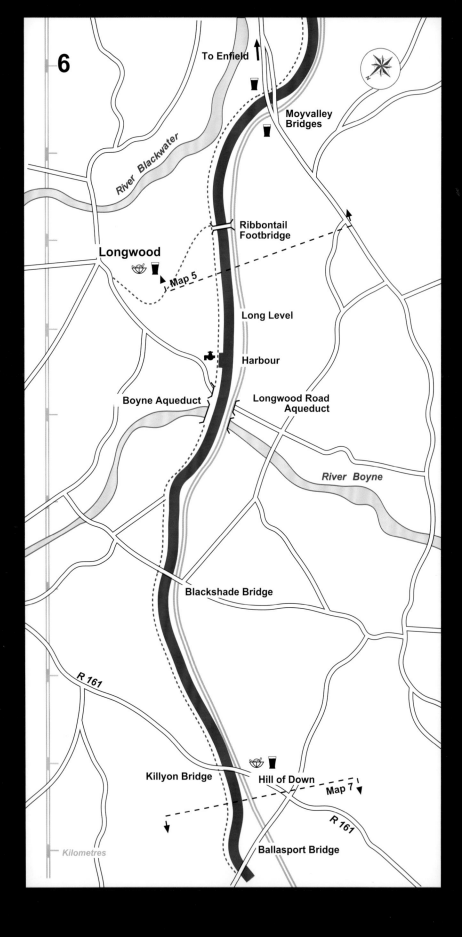

6

To Enfield

Moyvalley
Bridges

River Blackwater

Ribbontail
Footbridge

Longwood

Map 5

Long Level

Harbour

Boyne Aqueduct

Longwood Road
Aqueduct

River Boyne

Blackshade Bridge

R 161

Killyon Bridge

Hill of Down

Map 7

R 161

Kilometres

Ballasport Bridge

SECTION 6 – MOYVALLEY TO BALLASPORT BRIDGE

Route Description

This is a fine stretch of waterway. The canal crosses the Longwood Road Aqueduct and the impressive three-arched aqueduct over the River Boyne, with the railway viaduct nearby. From Hill of Down the canal is through more open country with typical hedgerows.

Facilities

Shops and pubs: Longwood (about 1.5 km; either along the boreen (narrow rural road) from Ribbontail Bridge or from Longwood Harbour).
Shop and Pub: Hill of Down.
Bus Service: Longwood, Bus Éireann service (very limited).
Water: Longwood Harbour.

History

In 1801 the canal company asked the newly elected Directors General of Inland Navigation for financial aid and they sent their engineer, John Brownrigg, to inspect the works. At this time the canal ended at the aqueduct over the Blackwater but the line was laid out across the Boyne and on towards Kinnegad. He said that the line was "as bad and as expensive as can be imagined" and the directors of the canal company were persuaded to alter the line to the north, away from Kinnegad. Some of the line had actually been excavated. It is possible to trace parts of the abandoned canal and to see the point at which it diverged from the present line about halfway between Blackshade Bridge and Hill of Down. A grant of £95,856 was given to the company with a proviso that the canal must be completed to Mullingar without further aid and that docks should be constructed at the junction with the River Liffey in Dublin.

The Ribbontail Footbridge was erected to facilitate people going to the nearby church but it is not clear how it received its name. There is possibly a connection with the Ribbonmen, (an illegal organisation whose aim was to protect the interests of the working classes) who are said to have congregated around the bridge when they were active in the area. The bridge was restored by the Longwood Branch of the RCAG.

A major breach of the embankment, east of the Longwood Road Aqueduct, occurred in June 1993. Its repair over the following months by the OPW was the biggest restoration project on the canal in any single location.

When the canal was in commercial use, the harbour beside the Longwood Road Aqueduct was known locally as "Boyne Dock".

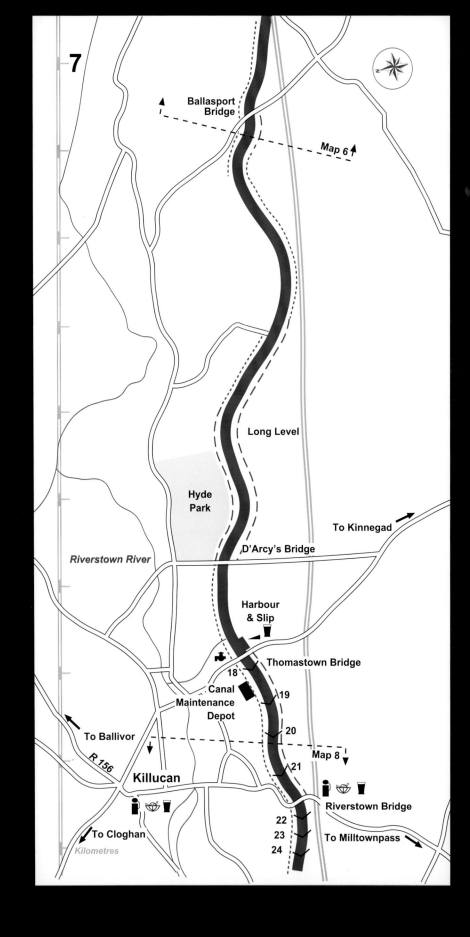

7

Ballasport Bridge

Map 6

Long Level

Hyde Park

To Kinnegad

Riverstown River

D'Arcy's Bridge

Harbour & Slip

Thomastown Bridge

18

Canal Maintenance Depot

19

To Ballivor

20

Map 8

R 156

21

Killucan

22

23

24

Riverstown Bridge

To Cloghan

To Milltownpass

Kilometres

SECTION 7 – BALLASPORT BRIDGE TO RIVERSTOWN BRIDGE

Route Description

At Hill of Down the railway line heads straight across a bog but the canal takes a more winding route. This can be a bleak and exposed section of canal until the wooded demense of Hyde Park is reached near D'Arcy's Bridge. At Thomastown the canal widens out into a large harbour fed by the Riverstown Supply before commencing the steep climb up to the summit level through a series of eight locks, spaced out at approximately 400 m intervals. From Thomastown to Riverstown Bridge there are now towpaths on both banks; that on the south side being driveable.

Facilities

Pub: Thomastown Harbour.
Shop, pub, garage: Killucan (about 2.4 km from Thomastown Bridge).
Shop, pub, garage: Riverstown Bridge.
Bus Service: Killucan (2.4 km north of Riverstown Bridge), Bus Éireann services 118,119 (very limited).
Slipway: Thomastown Harbour, access beside pub on south bank.
Water: Thomastown Harbour. Waterways Ireland Maintenance Depot and Office, located above 18th Lock, north bank. Tel:+353 (0)44 937 4940.

History

Having abandoned the line through Kinnegad, work continued on the new line to Thomastown and the canal was opened to here in 1805. One year earlier the rival canal, the Grand Canal, had been opened right through to the River Shannon. The old canal boats lying above D'Arcy's Bridge belong to the Leech family of Killucan, who were the last bye-traders working on the canal before it closed.

When, in 1985, the harbour at Thomastown was restored by the Killucan Branch of the RCAG, a new boat slipway was constructed on the south bank.

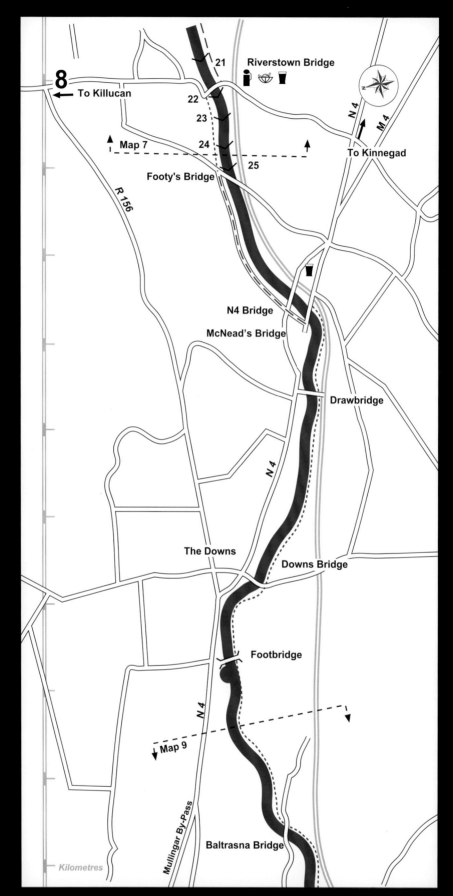

8

To Killucan

21

Riverstown Bridge

22

23

Map 7

24

25

Footy's Bridge

To Kinnegad

N4 Bridge

McNead's Bridge

Drawbridge

N 4

The Downs

Downs Bridge

Footbridge

N 4

Map 9

R 156

Mullingar By-Pass

Baltrasna Bridge

Kilometres

SECTION 8 – RIVERSTOWN BRIDGE TO BALTRASNA BRIDGE

Route Description

Continuing up the staircase, there is a towpath on the north bank only from Riverstown Bridge and the railway rejoins the canal. This is a very attractive stretch. The 25th Lock marks the start of the 24 km long Summit Level. About 1 km beyond McNead's Bridge is a lifting bridge giving access to a farm on the south bank. This bridge has to be operated by boaters and should always be left in the lowered position. Road, rail and canal continue close together as far as Down's Bridge but from here the railway follows a more southerly route into Mullingar whilst the canal twists its way between road and rail. For about 1.5 km either side of Baltrasna Bridge the canal passes through a narrow rock cutting reminiscent of the "Deep Sinking" through Carpenterstown but not as steep. Care should be taken here as in places there may be insufficient width for boats to pass each other.

Facilities

Shop, pub, garage: Riverstown Bridge.
Pub: McNead's Bridge.
Bus Service: Killucan (2.4 km north of Riverstown Bridge), (very limited).

History

Beside the towpath, just above 23rd Lock, is one of the few remaining milestones to be found along the banks of the canal. It indicates 43 miles from here to Broadstone Harbour in statute miles. Once again the engineers seem to have chosen a very difficult line for the canal approaching Mullingar. To preserve the level it was necessary to carve out a line for the canal through rock which proved very costly. The Summit Level as far as Mullingar was eventually opened to traffic in 1806 but the government grant had been long since exhausted and the company was once again facing financial difficulties. The Midland Great Western Railway Company, which had acquired the Royal Canal with a view to building the railway line along its route, completed its railway line to Mullingar in 1848. Although the railway company's administration of the canal was subject to a Government Board of Control, the canal inevitably did not prosper under railway management and its condition was allowed to deteriorate over the years.

A new road bridge, replacing McNead's Bridge, was finished in 1975. The original plans did not allow full navigational clearance but, following representations from the Inland Waterways Association of Ireland (IWAI), Mr. Tully – the Minister for Local Government at the time – intervened and Westmeath County Council agreed to his request to alter the plans. This was a turning point in the campaign for the restoration of the canal and, thereafter, permission for non-navigable bridges over the canal was refused.

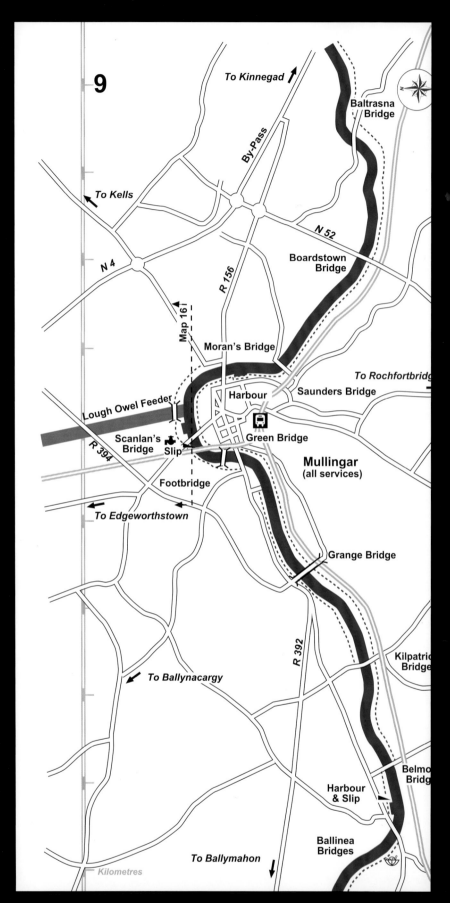

9

To Kinnegad ↑

Baltrasna
Bridge

By-Pass

To Kells

N 52

N 4

R 156

Boardstown
Bridge

Map 16

Moran's Bridge

Lough Owel Feeder

To Rochfortbridge

Harbour

Saunders Bridge

Scanlan's
Bridge

Slip

R 394

Green Bridge

Mullingar
(all services)

Footbridge

To Edgeworthstown

Grange Bridge

R 392

Kilpatric
Bridge

To Ballynacargy

Belmo
Bridg

Harbour
& Slip

Ballinea
Bridges

To Ballymahon

Kilometres

SECTION 9 – BALTRASNA BRIDGE THROUGH MULLINGAR TO BALLINEA BRIDGE

Route Description

A short distance beyond Boardstown Bridge a feeder enters from the south through twin stone culverts, known locally as the "Pig's Nostril". There is a tendency for a silt bar to form in the channel, requiring regular dredging to maintain a navigable depth. Passing the small harbour at Piper's Boreen, the canal continues in a great loop to the north of Mullingar before leaving to the south-west. Halfway around this loop, and just before the main harbour, the supply feeder enters from Lough Owel, 3.6 km to the north. This supply feeder is navigable by dinghy or canoe for approximately 2 km upstream from the harbour and is also a pleasant and interesting walk. (See section 16, The Lough Owel Feeder).

The extensive harbour at Mullingar is divided in two by Scanlan's Bridge. There is also a dry dock opening off the harbour (east side) and a boat slipway west of the bridge. Leaving town, the canal meets up with the railway again but at Ballinea Bridge they finally part company as the railway line turns south for Athlone. There is another boat slipway into this level at Ballinea Harbour (north bank).

Facilities

All Services: Mullingar.
Shop: Ballinea Bridge (about 500 m to the south).
Railway Station: Mullingar.
Bus Services: Mullingar, Bus Éireann services 22, 23, 70, 115, 116, 117, 118, 119, 447.
Slipways: Mullingar Harbour, north bank, west of Scanlan's Bridge. Ballinea Harbour, north bank.
Dry Dock: Mullingar Harbour.
Fuel: Mullingar, petrol & diesel at filling station beside Moran's Bridge.
Water: Mullingar Harbour.

History

Once again there was controversy about the line the canal should take at Mullingar. The original line was marked out and valued to run south of the town but this route involved a high embankment and so the northerly route was adopted following the contour of the land. Urban development in the Mullingar area in recent years has resulted in increased demand for potable (or drinking) water. Abstraction from Lough Owel has steadily increased – the water has a unique quality due to its small catchment area. There is also a fish farm drawing water from the feeder. The water entering the feeder is controlled at a sluice-house at the point where the feeder leaves the lake. Waterways Ireland and Westmeath County Council are engaged in securing an alternative water supply for the canal.

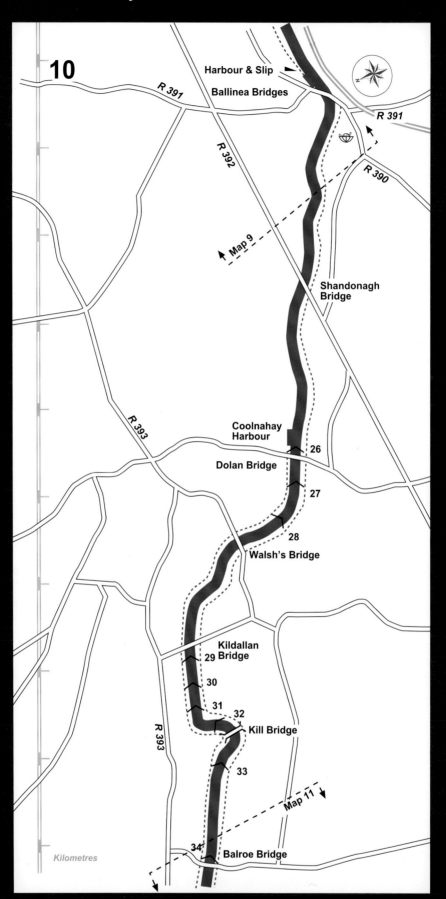

10

Harbour & Slip
Ballinea Bridges

R 391

R 392

R 391

R 390

Map 9

Shandonagh
Bridge

R 393

Coolnahay
Harbour

26

Dolan Bridge

27

28

Walsh's Bridge

Kildallan
29 Bridge

30

31

32

Kill Bridge

R 393

33

Map 11

34

Balroe Bridge

Kilometres

SECTION 10 – BALLINEA BRIDGE TO 34TH LOCK NEAR BALLYNACARGY

Route Description

This is a very attractive section of the canal. The descent from Coolnahay towards the Shannon is rather more gradual than the climb up to the summit from Thomastown, the first ten locks being spaced out over the 8 km to Ballynacargy. From Coolnahay the canal twists its way towards the Inny Valley seeking to avoid high ground. By doing so it also avoids most forms of habitation other than the occasional house or farm. Thus once Ballinea is left behind, there are no facilities along this stretch of waterway.

Facilities

Shop: Ballinea Bridge (about 500 m to the south).

History

At Ballinea there is an interesting example of a "skew bridge", of which there are only two on the Royal Canal, the other being Ballasport Bridge, which is only very slightly skewed. There are engineering difficulties about designing the courses of skew humpbacked bridges and the Romans were probably the first to overcome these problems. Early canal engineers usually

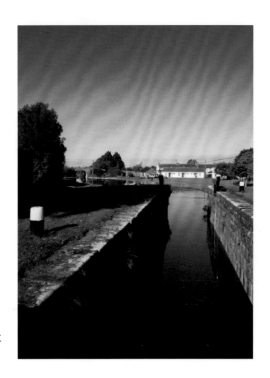

took the easy way out and realigned the roads to cross the canal at right angles. The canal was completed to Coolnahay by 1809 but by this time the company was heavily in debt. The small surplus revenue coming in from the part of the canal that was operational was insufficient to pay the interest on the debt let alone continue work on the canal. In addition, controversy had arisen with the Grand Canal Company about the line the canal was to follow to the Shannon. Any deviation from the line actually authorised by parliament, which threatened the trade on the Grand Canal, was strongly resisted by this company. Finally, the government was asked to intervene in the dispute and this led to a decision to inquire into the financial affairs of both companies. It became obvious that the Royal Canal Company was no longer in a position to complete the canal and so it was decided that the company should be dissolved and the canal completed using public funds. The government felt that it would be an even greater loss to the country to leave the canal in an unfinished state after so much public and private money had been invested in the scheme. In 1813 the Directors General of Inland Navigation took over control of the concern with instructions to complete the canal to the Shannon.

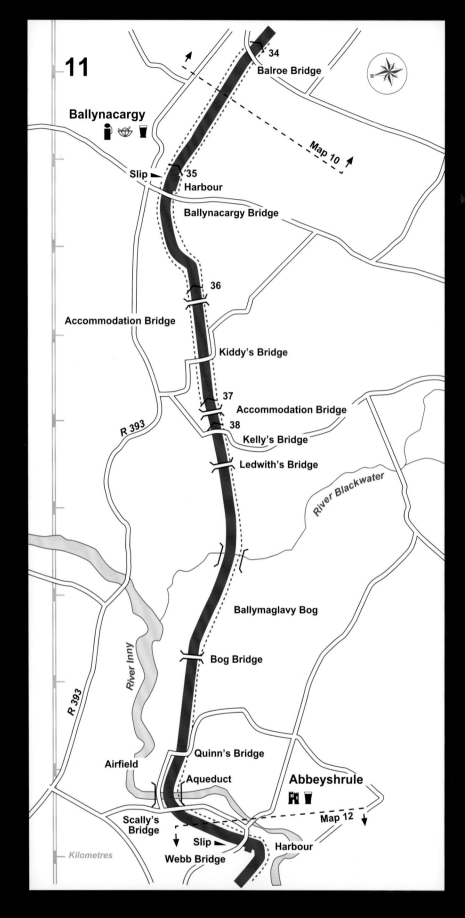

11

Ballynacargy

Balroe Bridge
34

Slip
'35
Harbour

Ballynacargy Bridge

Map 10

36

Accommodation Bridge

Kiddy's Bridge

37
Accommodation Bridge
38
Kelly's Bridge

R 393

Ledwith's Bridge

River Blackwater

Ballymaglavy Bog

River Inny

Bog Bridge

R 393

Quinn's Bridge

Airfield

Aqueduct

Abbeyshrule

Map 12

Scally's
Bridge

Slip
Webb Bridge

Harbour

Kilometres

SECTION 11 – 34TH LOCK NEAR BALLYNACARGY TO RIVER INNY AQUEDUCT AND ABBEYSHRULE

Route Description

Ballynacargy owes its existence largely to the canal and was an important trading centre. Leaving here there are three more locks before the canal enters Ballymaglavy Bog. It is a pleasant but exposed journey across the bog. After traversing the bog the canal enters County Longford, and crosses the River Inny by an imposing aqueduct that was underpinned several years ago when the Inny drainage scheme was being carried out. Abbeyshrule Airfield is located beside the canal on the north bank just before the canal crosses the river. After crossing the Inny the canal turns sharply to the south and follows the river valley into Abbeyshrule.

Facilities

Shops, pubs, garage: Ballynacargy.
Bus Service: Ballynacargy, Bus Éireann service 119 (Saturday only).
Pubs, restaurant: Abbeyshrule.
Slipways: Ballynacargy Harbour, north bank and Abbeyshrule, north bank, east of Webb Bridge.
Water: Ballynacargy Harbour.
Toilets: Ballynacargy Harbour.

History

Faced with the daunting task of completing the canal, the Directors General of Inland Navigation entered into a contract with an engineering firm, Henry, Mullins & MacMahon, to carry out the entire extension to the Shannon for £145,000. The plaque on the Whitworth Aqueduct over the Inny is difficult to decipher. It reads:

"This Aqueduct with the entire Royal Canal Extension 24.5 miles in length, having 21 Locks, 38 Bridges and 40 Tunnels, with several extensive Harbours, Quays and other Works of Masonry was designed by John Killaly Esq., Engineer to the Directors General of Inland Navigation and executed under their Direction in the short space of 3 years by the Undertakers, Henry, Mullins & MacMahon." (The mileage is in Irish Miles – 2240 yards, 2048 m).

At Abbeyshrule, as its name denotes, the remains of a Cistercian Abbey are to be found. Follow the signpost through the graveyard and through two further gates. The place was colonised from Mellifont Abbey around 1150 AD but the earliest buildings date from around 1200. The oldest buildings are the chancel, altered in the sixteenth century to form a chapel, and the tower, which was later blocked by a wall with three compartments. The other tower was built in post-Reformation times. There is an interesting shaft of a High Cross in the graveyard which has a strange horseshoe device on it.

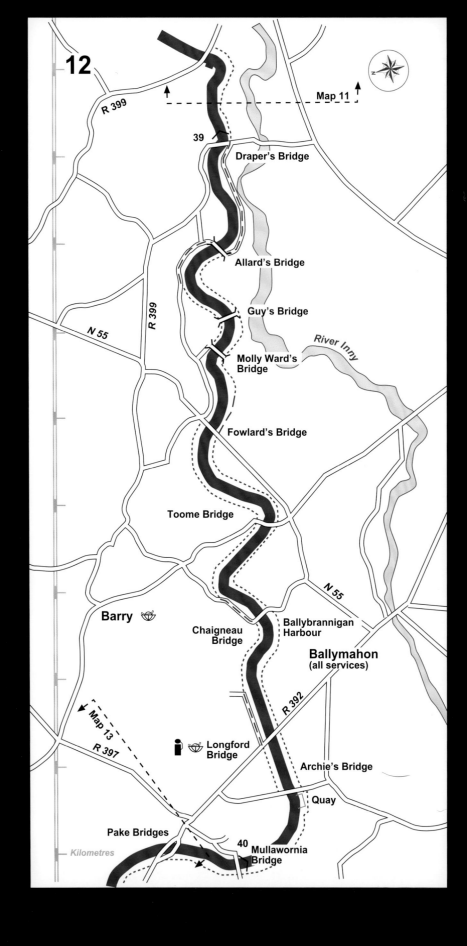

12

R 399

Map 11

39

Draper's Bridge

Allard's Bridge

R 399

N 55

Guy's Bridge

Molly Ward's
Bridge

River Inny

Fowlard's Bridge

Toome Bridge

Barry

N 55

Chaigneau
Bridge

Ballybrannigan
Harbour

Ballymahon
(all services)

R 392

Map 13

R 397

Longford
Bridge

Archie's Bridge

Quay

Pake Bridges

40

Kilometres

Mullawornia
Bridge

SECTION 12 – ABBEYSHRULE TO PAKE BRIDGE NEAR BALLYMAHON

Route Description

The level from 39th Lock is the longest on the western end of the canal, extending for more than 11 km. The canal follows the contours of the Inny Valley and is undoubtedly the most winding section of the whole line. As far as Archie's Bridge there are now towpaths on both banks. For the first 6.5 km the canal is narrow and enclosed with high hedgerows so that the nearby river is only visible occasionally.

Passing under Chaigneau Bridge, known locally as Brannigan Bridge, the canal opens out into Ballybrannigan Harbour where there is a large store, and the passage-boat ticket office, recently restored by the Ballymahon Branch of the RCAG. This stretch of canal around Ballymahon is through more open country and parts of the canal are embanked. At Archie's Bridge there is a quay and the remains of two large stores. From here the canal curves around Mullawornia Hill following the contours. At this point the canal is only about 3 km from the River Shannon at Lough Ree but instead of continuing west in the Inny Valley, it takes a sharp turn to the north. Emerging from a cutting the canal enters 40th Lock, Mullawornia, and is carried along a rocky escarpment with the rock rising sheer above the east bank and falling away almost vertically on the opposite side. An extensive stone quarrying operation has eaten away a large portion of Mullawornia Hill. As can be imagined, there are excellent views towards Lough Ree.

Facilities

Shop: Barry (about 2 km from Toome Bridge or Ballybrannigan Harbour).
All Services: Ballymahon (about 1.5 km from Toome Bridge, Ballybrannigan Harbour or Longford Bridge).
Shop, garage: R392 Lanesborough road, approximately 400 m west of Longford Bridge.
Bus Service: Ballymahon, Bus Éireann services 65, 73, 271, 466.

History

Although the harbour and passage boat station were at Ballybrannigan Harbour, Toome Bridge was the place where passengers alighted to connect with Bianconi's cars to Athlone. Bianconi was Ireland's principal operator of horse-drawn coaches which were frequently referred to as "cars". There were quite a number of places along the route of the canal where coaching establishments provided connecting services. In the 1830s over 40,000 passengers were carried per year on the canal and the tonnage of goods rose to a peak of 100,000 tons per annum in the 1840s.

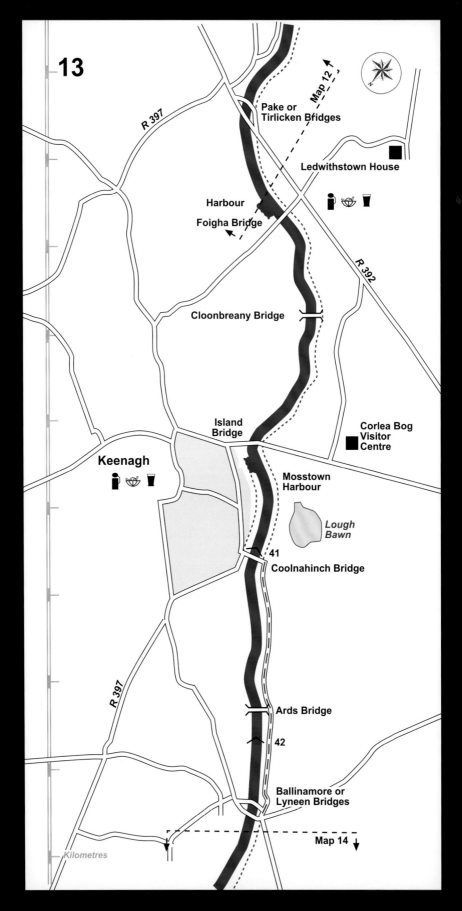

13

Pake or
Tirlicken Bridges

Map 12

Ledwithstown House

R 397

Harbour

Foigha Bridge

R 392

Cloonbreany Bridge

Island
Bridge

Corlea Bog
Visitor
Centre

Keenagh

Mosstown
Harbour

Lough
Bawn

41

Coolnahinch Bridge

R 397

Ards Bridge

42

Ballinamore or
Lyneen Bridges

Map 14

Kilometres

SECTION 13 – PAKE BRIDGE TO LYNEEN BRIDGE

Route Description

Re-crossing under the Ballymahon to Lanesborough Road at Pake Bridge, the canal continues in a northerly direction via Foigha Harbour to Cloonbreany Bridge, beyond which it widens out considerably as it passes across the windswept expanse of Cloonbreany Bog before reaching Island Bridge and Mosstown Harbour. Beyond the harbour, which is within easy walking distance of Keenagh village, the canal enters a shallow cutting alongside the dense woodland of Mosstown Estate which continues as far as Coolnahinch Lock. From here to Lyneen Bridge the canal is accompanied by a road which has superseded the towpath on the west bank.

Facilities

Shop, pub, garage: Foigha Cross Roads, R392 (about 300 m south of Foigha Bridge).
Shops, pubs, petrol: Keenagh (about 1.2 km from Island bridge).
Bus Service: Keenagh, Bus Éireann services 466, 468 (very limited).

History

The Grand Canal Company opposed any suggestion that the Royal Canal should terminate in Lough Ree, a little over 3 km from Mullawornia. The government agreed that the purpose of the canal was to serve the north Shannon and, in particular, to provide a route for Lough Allen coal. Moreover, it was thought to be impractical to terminate the canal in a large lake where adverse weather conditions could hold up traffic for long periods. Thus the canal continues for another 19 km to the junction with the Shannon.

Between the canal and the Shannon lies a vast tract of bog over which, from as far back as 3,500 BC, a large network of wooden tracks was laid. When, in the 1960s, Bord na Móna brought its industry to Corlea Bog these trackways began to be uncovered. A preserved portion of the trackways and numerous important artefacts are on display in the Corlea Bog Visitor Centre about 1.5 km west of Island Bridge.

Mosstown House, the home of the Kingston family, was demolished in 1962 but visitors to Keenagh village can admire the clock tower (1875) with its clock still in working order. Also of interest are the entrance to the estate through a 1.6 km long avenue of lime trees planted in 1850; the eagle-topped piers at the White Gate, built by Belgian refugees after the first World War; and the restored Pigeon House, the only one of its kind in the country.

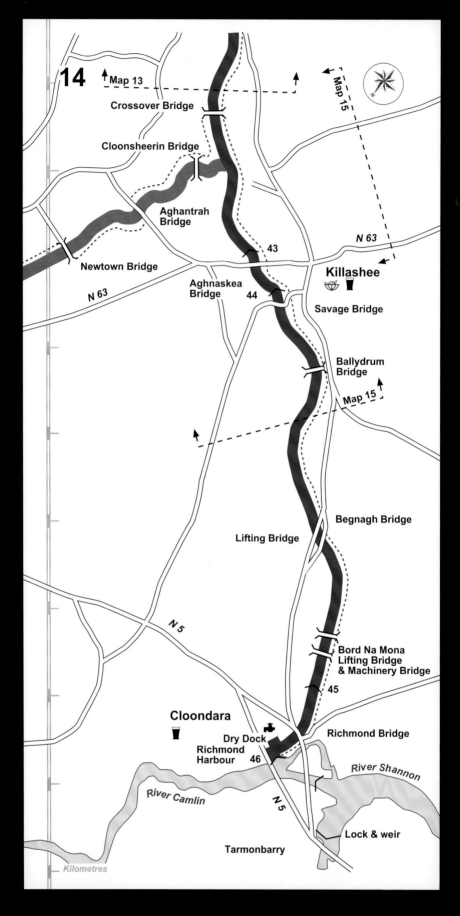

14

Map 13

Crossover Bridge

Cloonsheerin Bridge

Aghantrah Bridge

Newtown Bridge

N 63

Aghnaskea Bridge

43

44

Map 15

N 63

Killashee

Savage Bridge

Ballydrum Bridge

Map 15

Begnagh Bridge

Lifting Bridge

N 5

Bord Na Mona Lifting Bridge & Machinery Bridge

45

Cloondara

Dry Dock Richmond Harbour

46

Richmond Bridge

River Shannon

River Camlin

N 5

Lock & weir

Tarmonbarry

Kilometres

SECTION 14 – LYNEEN BRIDGE TO RICHMOND HARBOUR, CLOONDARA, JUNCTION WITH THE RIVER SHANNON

Route Description

Along this section, the canal is hemmed in by dense hedgerows as far as Crossover Bridge, beyond which it enters more open country as it approaches the junction with the non-navigable Longford Branch and continues on to the 43rd Lock, near Killashee village. Shortly after the 44th Lock the canal enters Begnagh Bog. Beside the original Begnagh Bridge is a lifting bridge carrying the Killashee to Cloondara road across the canal. The bridge opens automatically and should be approached slowly to allow time for the road barriers to be lowered and the bridge to lift before the green light appears. Approximately 1.5 km beyond Begnagh Bridge the Bord na Móna light-railway crosses the canal via another lifting bridge (non-automatic) which is normally kept in the open position. The second Bord na Móna bridge alongside is a high-level machinery crossing. After passing through the 45th Lock at Rinnmount the canal shortly enters the terminus at Richmond Harbour.

The 46th Lock, at the far end of the harbour, leads into the Camlin River which connects with the River Shannon in Lough Forbes or, by passing down a short length of canal and through the old Shannon Navigation Lock, below the weir at Tarmonbarry. The dry dock at Richmond Harbour can be availed of by arrangement with Waterways Ireland – contact the Royal Canal Depot at Thomastown, located just above the 18th Lock, Killucan.
Tel. +353 (0)44 937 4940.

Facilities

Shop, pubs: Killashee (west of the canal from 43rd or 44th Lock).
Pubs: Cloondara.
Bus Service: Killashee, Bus Éireann services 425, 467, (both infrequent). Tarmonbarry, N5 road 1.5 km north of Richmond Harbour, Bus Éireann services 22, 451.
Dry Dock: Richmond Harbour.
Water: Richmond Harbour.

History

The canal was completed to Richmond Harbour in 1817 and in the following year the whole concern was handed over to the newly constituted New Royal Canal Company with a government appointed Board of Control to keep an eye on its affairs. However, the expected trade from the north Shannon did not materialise even after the completion of the Lough Allen Canal in 1821. The total cost of the canal from Dublin had been about £1.5 million and it had taken nearly thirty years to complete. In the 1830s the distillery at Cloondara was producing some 70,000 gallons of whiskey a year and employing about 70 people; it subsequently became a cornmill and was recently converted into apartments. There are some interesting graveslabs in the graveyard beside the church in Cloondara. This was the site of an early monastery and hospice.

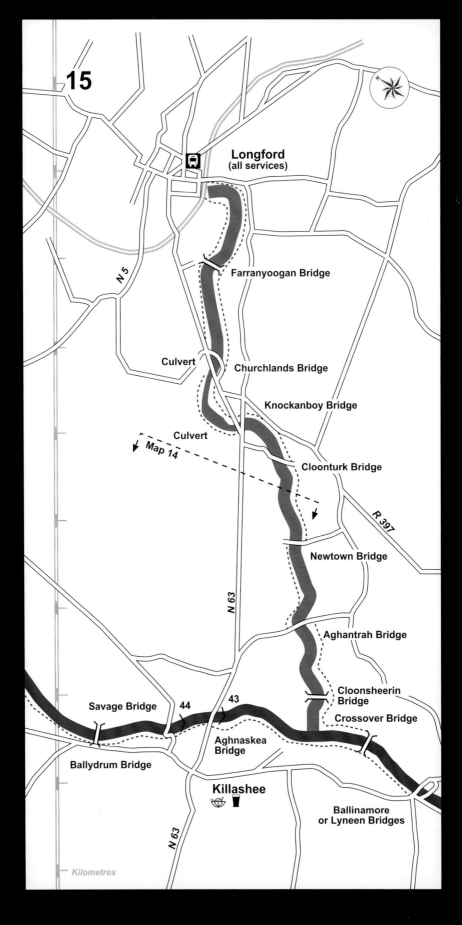

15

Longford
(all services)

Farranyoogan Bridge

Culvert

Churchlands Bridge

Knockanboy Bridge

Culvert

Map 14

Cloonturk Bridge

N 5

N 63

R 397

Newtown Bridge

Aghantrah Bridge

Cloonsheerin
Bridge

Savage Bridge

44

43

Crossover Bridge

Aghnaskea
Bridge

Ballydrum Bridge

Killashee

N 63

Ballinamore
or Lyneen Bridges

Kilometres

SECTION 15 – THE LONGFORD BRANCH (NOT NAVIGABLE)

Description

The Longford Branch is dry except for the section between Farranyoogan Bridge and Longford. It is an attractive walk, much of it tree-lined. The final part of the canal where it passed under the railway and opened out into a harbour has been filled in and the branch now terminates south of the railway. The last 1.5 km was re-watered by constructing a dam below Farranyoogan Bridge and has been developed as an amenity for the town. A supply of water is assured because the upper part of the branch is fed by springs.

Facilities

All Services: Longford.
Railway Station: Longford.
Bus service: Longford, Bus Éireann services 22, 23, 65, 73, 116, 119, 425, 451, 466, 467, 468 469.

History

Lower Lyneen or Crossover Bridge, as its name denotes, was built at the same time as the Longford Branch to enable the towing horses to cross to the other bank to gain access to the branch towpath. The branch was officially opened in January 1830. Because part of the canal was through boggy terrain the contractor had to contend with great engineering problems. In addition, local people from Killashee and Richmond Harbour were strongly opposed to the building of the branch which they saw as a threat to their trade. Both before and after the opening the canal works were breached several times maliciously. The fears of the people were realised, Longford became the passenger boat terminus and also the centre for the trade boats

Restoration

The branch has been dredged and the banks have been cleared by way of Social Employment Schemes sponsored by Longford County Council and the Longford Branch of the RCAG. Although Longford Harbour was filled in over 40 years ago, the site remained unused and unadorned until 1996 when it became a temporary car park. A disused indoor swimming pool sits astride the filled-in canal at the entrance to the harbour. If the harbour were to be re-excavated, all of the original stonework is in situ under the compacted infill. A new swing bridge would be needed where the railway crossed at low level and there is a problem of a recently built house encroaching on the line of the canal midway between the railway and the harbour. There are only four locks between Longford and the River Shannon. Waterways Ireland is charged with undertaking a feasibility study into the restoration of the Longford Branch.

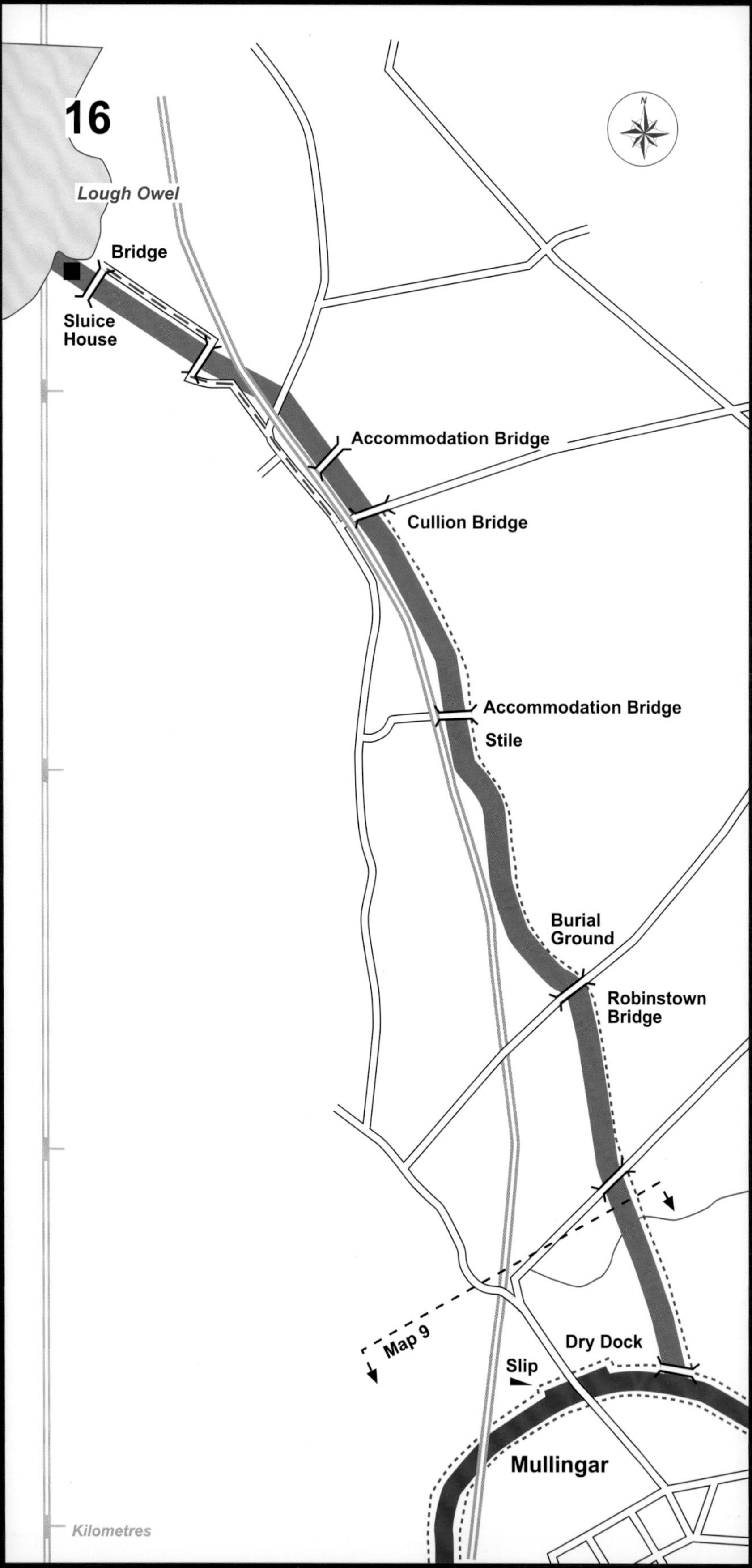

16

Lough Owel

Bridge

Sluice House

Accommodation Bridge

Cullion Bridge

Accommodation Bridge

Stile

Burial Ground

Robinstown Bridge

Map 9

Dry Dock

Slip

Mullingar

Kilometres

SECTION 16 – THE LOUGH OWEL FEEDER (NOT NAVIGABLE)

Lough Owel is connected with the Royal Canal via a 3.6 km channel or feeder. The feeder is much narrower and shallower than the canal itself and never formed part of the navigation. At one time, however, it was possible to navigate the full length of the channel in a small boat and an account of such a trip, made in 1946, is to be found in *"Green and Silver"* by Tom Rolt who, along with Charles Hadfield and Robert Aikman, founded the Inland Waterways Association in Britain just a few weeks before this trip was made. Such a trip is no longer possible as a number of obstacles now bar the way but a journey from Mullingar Harbour for approximately half the length of the feeder is still feasible in a dinghy or canoe.

It is, however, possible to walk alongside the feeder for virtually the whole distance. The path commences on the east side of the beautifully proportioned towpath bridge over the mouth of the feeder at Mullingar Harbour. After about 400 m, it crosses a tributary of the River Brosna. There is ample headroom under both the first road bridge and under Robinstown Bridge, which was widened a few years ago. At the same time, the low-level pipes on the upstream side that obstructed the channel were removed. Keep a look-out for an interesting gateway on the right. A stone lintel carries the inscription "Mullingar Union" and the gateway is the entrance into an old burial ground. A short distance further the railway line joins the feeder on the west bank, but whereas the railway follows a gentle curve the feeder takes a winding course and the west bank, between the two, is well wooded.

Shortly before reaching the first accommodation bridge which has lost its parapet walls, there is a stile to be crossed alongside which strands of barbed wire are stretched across the feeder channel, making this the limit of navigation by dinghy or canoe. (An accommodation bridge is a narrow bridge built by the canal company to accommodate land-owners/farmers whose lands were severed by the building of the canal). The wire across the channel is there for a purpose, as from here to the gate at the fish farm, cattle have access to the bank from an adjoining field and the feeder is their source of drinking water. Beyond this accommodation bridge, the feeder enters a cutting. At Cullion fish farm the channel has been culverted by water metering apparatus. The fish farm is licensed to abstract a maximum of 13.6 million litres of water per day from Lough Owel, via the Royal Canal feeder channel.

At Cullion Bridge it is necessary to follow the road for about 450 m (see map), rejoining the feeder channel where it emerges from under the railway line. Close to the lake, and sitting astride the channel, is the Royal Canal Sluice House. To the rear of the house can be seen the main sluice gate and the mechanism controlling the flow of water. This was one obstruction which even Rolt and his friends had to portage around! What a pity though that one cannot make a return journey in the way they did when, having transferred the dinghy from Lough Owel to the feeder, *"we all clambered aboard and floated serenely on the current down to the canal, occasionally crouching in the bottom of the boat as we went under a culvert"*.

DISTANCE TABLE

	Km	Section No
Main Line		
Dublin North Wall, lifting bridges and sea lock (Start of Spencer Dock)	0.00	1a
Mayor Street Bridge	0.20	1a
Sheriff Street drawbridge (Spencer Bridge)	0.30	1a
High level railway bridges	0.90	1a
Railway loop line, lifting bridge (End of Spencer Dock)	1.05	1a
Newcomen Bridge, North Strand Road and 1st Lock	1.15	1a
Clarke Bridge, Summerhill Parade	1.35	1b
Clonliffe Bridge, Russell Street	1.85	1b
Binns Bridge, Drumcondra Road and 2nd Lock (double)	2.25	1b
3rd Lock (double)	2.55	1b
4th Lock (double)	2.80	1b
Junction with Broadstone Branch (now filled in)	3.00	1b
Westmoreland Bridge, Cross Guns and 5th Lock (double)	3.15	1b
6th Lock (double)	3.45	1b
Railway Bridge and 7th Lock, Liffey Junction	4.65	1b
Hamilton Bridge, Broomebridge	5.30	1b
Reilly's Bridge and 8th Lock	5.85	1b
9th Lock	6.45	1b
Longford Bridge, Dublin City-Fingal county boundary and 10th Lock (double)	7.50	1b
11th Lock (double)	8.95	1b
New River Road Bridge	9.35	1b
Ranelagh Bridge	9.55	1b
Blanchardstown by-pass Bridge	9.65	1b
M50 Motorway Aqueduct	9.75	1b
Blanchardstown by-pass bridge	9.80	1b
Talbot Bridge and 12th Lock (double), Blanchardstown	9.90	1b
Granard Bridge, Castleknock Road	10.20	2
Kirkpatrick Bridge, Carpenterstown	11.75	2
Dr. Troy Bridge	12.45	2
Kennan Bridge, Porterstown	12.65	2
Callaghan Bridge, Clonsilla	13.85	2
Railway Bridge	14.70	2
Pakenham Bridge, Barberstown	15.10	2
Collins Bridge, Coldblow	16.90	2
Fingal-Kildare county boundary, Confey amenity area and boat slip	17.95	2
Cope Bridge	18.85	2
Ryewater Aqueduct	20.25	2
Leixlip Spa and Louisa Bridge	20.70	2

Matt Goff or Collinstown Bridge	21.65	3
Deey Bridge and 13th Lock	22.30	3
Carton Wharf and Pike Bridge	24.15	3
Mullen Bridges	26.30	3
Maynooth Harbour, boat slip and footbridge	26.45	3
Bond Bridge	26.95	3
Jackson Bridge and 14th Lock	28.65	3
Bailey's Bridge (accommodation)	30.00	3
Chamber's Bridge and 15th Lock, The Maws	30.75	3
Kilcock Harbour, Shaw's Bridge and 16th Lock (double)	32.40	4
Allen or Spin Bridge	33.45	4
Kildare-Meath county boundary	35.25	4
Ryewater feeder, McLoughlin's Bridge, 17th Lock (double)	36.20	4
Meath-Kildare county boundary	39.65	4
Cloncurry Bridge and Kildare-Meath county boundary	42.10	5
Enfield Bridge and amenity area	45.15	5
Enfield Harbour and boat slip	45.30	5
River Blackwater Aqueduct and Meath-Kildare county boundary	48.85	5
Kilmore Bridge	49.65	5
Moyvalley Bridges	51.40	5
Ribbontail Bridge (footbridge) and stop gates	53.40	6
Kildare-Meath county boundary	53.75	6
Longwood Harbour and Longwood Road Aqueduct	55.20	6
River Boyne Aqueduct	55.45	6
Blackshade Bridge	57.60	6
Hill of Down or Killyon Bridge	60.10	6
Ballasport Bridge	61.40	6
Meath-Westmeath county boundary	63.80	7
D'Arcy's Bridge	67.25	7
Riverstown feeder, Thomastown Harbour and Bridge and 18th Lock	68.55	7
19th Lock	69.10	7
20th Lock	69.50	7
21st Lock	70.00	7
Riverstown Bridge and 22nd Lock, Killucan	70.40	7
23rd Lock	70.80	8
24th Lock	71.30	8
25th Lock and start of summit level	71.50	8
Footy's Bridge	71.70	8
N4 road bridge	73.65	8
McNead's or Heathstown Bridge	73.70	8
Lifting accommodation bridge	74.65	8
Downs Bridge	77.00	8
Footbridge	77.90	8
Baltrasna Bridge	80.45	8

Boardstown Bridge	82.05	9
Saunder's Bridge	83.75	9
Harbour (Piper's Boreen)	84.05	9
Moran's Bridge	84.55	9
Lough Owel feeder	85.30	9
Mullingar Harbour, dry dock, Scanlan's Bridge and boat slip	85.50	9
Railway Bridge	85.85	9
Footbridge	86.10	9
The Green Bridge	86.30	9
Grange Bridge	87.95	9
Kilpatrick Bridge	89.55	9
Belmont Bridge	90.90	9
Ballinea Harbour and Ballinea Bridges	91.55	9
Shandonagh Bridges	93.95	10
Coolnahay Harbour, 26th Lock, end of summit level and Dolan Bridge	96.05	10
27th Lock	96.45	10
28th Lock	96.95	10
Walsh's Bridge (accommodation bridge)	97.50	10
Kildallan Bridge	98.95	10
29th Lock	99.10	10
30th Lock	99.45	10
31st Lock	99.70	10
32nd Lock and Kill Bridge (accommodation bridge)	100.40	10
33rd Lock	100.95	10
34th Lock and Balroe Bridge	102.15	10
Balroe feeder	102.65	11
35th Lock, Ballynacargy Harbour	104.00	11
Ballynacargy Bridge	104.20	11
36th Lock and accommodation bridge	105.65	11
Kiddy's Bridge	106.20	11
37th Lock and accommodation bridge	106.85	11
38th Lock and Kelly's Bridge	107.15	11
Ledwith's Bridge (accommodation bridge)	107.70	11
Blackwater River (passes under canal via 3.7 m wide tunnel)	108.60	11
Bog Bridge (accommodation bridge)	110.00	11
Westmeath-Longford county boundary	110.40	11
Quinn's Bridge (accommodation bridge)	111.25	11
Whitworth Aqueduct over River Inny	111.85	11
Scally's Bridge	112.00	11
Boat slip, Webb Bridge and Abbeyshrule harbour	112.80	11
39th Lock and Draper's Bridge, Tinnelick	114.30	12
Allard's Bridge (accommodation bridge)	115.95	12
Guy's Bridge (accommodation bridge)	117.05	12
Molly Ward's Bridge (accommodation bridge)	117.60	12

Fowlard's or Cloonard Bridge	118.65	12
Toome Bridge	120.25	12
Chaigneau Bridge and Ballybrannigan Harbour, Ballymahon	121.90	12
Longford Bridge	123.40	12
Archie's Bridge and Quay	124.20	12
40th Lock and accommodation bridge, Mullawornia	125.60	12
Pake or Terlicken Bridges	126.45	12
Foigha Harbour and Bridge	127.90	13
Cloonbreany Bridge (accommodation bridge)	129.50	13
Island Bridge and Mosstown Harbour, Keenagh	131.35	13
41st Lock and Coolnahinch Bridge	132.80	13
Ards Bridge (accommodation bridge)	134.60	13
42nd Lock, Ards	135.00	13
Lyneen or Ballinamore Bridges	135.90	13
Lower Lyneen or Crossover Bridge	137.00	14
Junction with Longford Branch, Cloonsheerin	137.75	14
43rd Lock and Aghnaskea Bridge, Killashee	139.10	14
Killashee Harbour, 44th Lock and Savage Bridge	139.75	14
Ballydrum Bridge (accommodation bridge)	140.70	14
Begnagh lifting bridge and Begnagh Bridge	142.90	14
Bord na Móna railway lifting bridge and machinery bridge	144.35	14
45th Lock, Rinnmount	144.80	14
Richmond Bridge, Richmond Harbour and dry dock, Cloondara	145.45	14
46th Lock, leading into Camlin River	145.60	14

Longford Branch

Cloonsheerin, junction with Main Line	0.00	15
Cloonsheerin Bridge (accommodation bridge)	0.30	15
Aghantrah Bridge	1.60	15
Newtown Bridge (accommodation bridge)	3.05	15
Cloonturk Bridge (accommodation bridge)	4.20	15
Knockanboy Bridge and culverted road crossing	4.85	15
Churchlands Bridge and culverted road crossing	5.80	15
Farranyoogan Bridge (accommodation bridge)	7.10	15
New terminus south of railway	8.35	15
Longford harbour (infilled)	8.50	15

WATERWAYS IRELAND

Mission Statement

Waterways Ireland is the guardian of Ireland's inland navigations. Our mission is to provide a high quality recreational environment centred on the inland waterways of Ireland in our care, for the use and benefit of everyone.

Background

Waterways Ireland, the largest of the North/South Implementation Bodies, is responsible for the management, maintenance, development and restoration of the inland navigable waterway system throughout the island, principally for recreational purposes. It is currently responsible for the following waterways:-

- Barrow Navigation;
- Erne System
- Grand Canal;
- Lower Bann Navigation;
- Royal Canal;
- Shannon-Erne Waterway; and
- Shannon Navigation.

Waterways Ireland's remit was extended in 2007 by the North/South Ministerial Council, to include responsibility for the restoration of the section of the Ulster Canal between Clones and Upper Lough Erne, and, following restoration, for the management, maintenance, and development of this waterway principally for recreational purposes.

Funding

Waterways Ireland is funded jointly by both jurisdictions, with 15% of current funding provided by the Northern Ireland Assembly and 85% by the Irish Government, reflecting the present distribution of the navigable waterways.

Capital development programmes are funded separately in each jurisdiction. Waterways Ireland continues to progress works under the National Development Plan 2007 to 2013, as part of its waterways programme. It also carries out a separate capital development programme in Northern Ireland funded by the Department of Culture, Arts and Leisure (DCAL).

Organisation

Waterways Ireland Headquarters is based at 2 Sligo Road, Enniskillen, Co.Fermanagh. The waterways are divided into three Regions:-

Eastern   Royal and Grand Canals and Barrow Navigation,

Western   Shannon Navigation and

Northern   Shannon-Erne Waterway, Erne System and Lower Bann Navigation.

Regional Offices are located at Dublin, Scarriff and Carrick-on-Shannon respectively. There are also several depots and offices along the various navigations.

Contact details for all offices and further information and can be obtained from the Waterways Ireland website at **www.waterwaysireland.org** or by emailing **info@waterwaysireland.org**

Royal Canal Restoration Project

Since Waterways Ireland was established, restoration of the Royal Canal has been a priority project. During the years when the canal was abandoned some local authorities demolished the existing canal bridges and realigned the roads at low level. Also Bord na Móna had two low level bridges crossing the canal. In order to reopen the canal to navigation it has been necessary to upgrade these bridges or remove the low level crossings and replace them with bridges which can facilitate modern navigation and road traffic needs. One original bridge has been upgraded to meet modern needs, two new moving bridges have been constructed and five new high level fixed bridges have been constructed.

Marketing and Promotion

Waterways Ireland seeks to promote, market and develop the tourism and commercial potential of the inland waterways within its remit through a five-stranded strategy of:-
- Promoting greater use of the waterways
- Awareness creation
- Development of Waterways Ireland's Corporate Identity
- Working in partnership with other bodies and
- Building a platform for sustained market development.

Various mediums are employed including an award-winning website, a wide and varied range of promotional, navigational, historical and environmental publications, exhibiting at consumer events and through merchandising.

Waterways Ireland supports a wide range of festivals and events on or along the waterways within its remit under its annual Sponsorship Programme. Through its Joint Activities Programme, support is also given to larger waterway-based events, often organised in conjunction with local authorities, which serve to generate awareness of the recreational value of waterways among a diverse audience.

Partnership working is employed where possible to maximise effectiveness among tourism and development agencies. The Lakelands and Inland Waterways project is one such example, where a collaboration between Waterways Ireland, Failte Ireland, Fermanagh Lakeland Tourism, Tourism Ireland, the Northern Ireland Tourist Board and Shannon Development, is responsible for a marketing and product-development initiative for the lakelands and waterways region, stretching from Belleek in Co.Fermanagh to Limerick.

Waterways Ireland is also playing a leading role, along with key stakeholders, in shaping Development Plans for the waterways, with a view to identifying and realising the inherent potential for leisure, recreation and tourism opportunities.

THE INLAND WATERWAYS ASSOCIATION OF IRELAND

The Inland Waterways Association of Ireland (IWAI) is a voluntary body of inland waterways enthusiasts that advocate the use, maintenance, protection, restoration and improvement of the inland waterways of Ireland. For further information visit **www.iwai.ie** The association was founded in 1954 to campaign for the conservation and development of the waterways and in particular their preservation as working navigations. When the Shannon was almost totally undeveloped for pleasure boating, IWAI fought the building of low bridges, thus ensuring the development of the river as an asset for all to use and enjoy. In the 1960s IWAI successfully fought plans to close the Circular Line of the Grand Canal in Dublin. Later the association campaigned for the re-opening of the Ballinamore & Ballyconnell Canal (now the Shannon-Erne Waterway), the Naas line of the Grand Canal and the Ulster Canal.

In 1974 the IWAI commenced a "save the Royal Canal" campaign and the Royal Canal Amenity Group was formed.

IWAI is the voice of waterways users and enthusiasts. It represents the views of members to governments (NI & RoI), to Waterways Ireland and other navigation authorities, to local authorities and the range of statutory and state-sponsored bodies whose activities impinge on the waterways in one way or another.

Membership & Organisation

IWAI has over 4500 members mainly organised in branches associated with the major navigations across the island. Our membership is drawn from all walks of life and from people with a wide range of interests – boating, angling, walking, heritage, environment. Many of our members own and use boats on rivers, lakes and canals ranging from motor cruisers to jet-skis, from barges to sailing dinghies and RIBs to rowing boats.

The association is a company limited by guarantee and a registered charity (CHY no 10915). It is governed by a council made up of representatives of each of the local branches and directly elected officers and members. Day to day affairs are managed by an executive committee.

IWAI is not responsible for the navigation, for registering boats, for harbours or similar facilities. The authority that is responsible for the Shannon Navigation, Erne System, Barrow Navigation, Lower Bann Navigation, Grand Canal, Royal Canal and Shannon-Erne Waterway is Waterways Ireland.

Publications

The IWAI publishes "Inland Waterways News", a quarterly magazine, sent out free to all members. The magazine covers a wide range of topics of interest to waterways enthusiasts at local, national and international level. IWAI also publishes a number of waterways related books and guides. Our web-site is one of the largest single reference sources for waterways related material in Ireland and a major source of referrals for waterways related businesses, which brings local events, activities and developments into national perspective. Some of the branches bring out local newsletters. Our web site at **www.iwai.ie** is also packed with waterways related information and whether you are a boat enthusiast, historian, archaeologist, or fisherman you will find something here of interest.

Branches

IWAI has 20 branches: five in Northern Ireland, 14 in the Republic and one activity-based branch. Every member is affiliated to a local branch and each branch is represented on the national Council. The branches are:

NI: Lough Erne, River Bann and Lough Neagh, Coalisland, Lagan and Newry.

ROI: Athlone, Barrow, Belturbet, Boyle River, Boyne Navigation, Carrick-on-Shannon, Corrib, Dublin, Kildare, Lough Derg, North Barrow, Offaly, Shannon Harbour and Slaney

activity-based: Cruising Club

You can join whichever branch you wish. You can join on line at **www.iwai.ie/join**

Improvements & Restoration

Work parties and funds are raised to improve navigations and to restore derelict ones. Current projects include the Ulster Canal, Lagan Navigation, Coalisland Canal, Boyne Navigation and the Kilbeggan and Corbally lines of the Grand Canal.

Boat Rallies

IWAI organises rallies and other events including annual rallies on the Barrow (Easter), Dublin (May), the Erne (May), the Grand Canal (May & June), Shannon Harbour (June), the Corrib (July), the Shannon (July), Lough Derg (July). Some rallies hold competitions which help to raise standards of boatmanship, seaworthiness and safety afloat. IWAI look forward to holding many rallies on the restored canal.

Social Events

Land-based events such as film shows, discussions and lectures are organised on a range of waterways topics including, safety, vessel maintenance, navigation, first-aid and waterways heritage.

Member Services

IWAI provides a number of branded products and services for members. We also sell waterways-related books and navigation charts. IWAI members can avail of a superb competitive boat insurance scheme that is only available to members. Visit **www.shop.iwai.ie**

Corporate Membership

Corporate membership is available to businesses and bodies that wish to be recognised as supporting the national charity concerned with the conservation, restoration and use of the inland waterways. Corporate members will receive a Corporate Investment Certificate which they can display in their offices to their customers and visitors so they may see that you are a friend of the Inland Waterways Association of Ireland and care about Ireland's waterways.

Public Relations and Communications

Each branch has a Public Relations Officer and the National IWAI PRO can be contacted at **pro@iwai.ie**

Email Discussion Forum

Why not sign up for our waterways mailing list discussion group at **www.iwai.ie**. There you will meet folk who enjoy talking about life on our waterways. Generally, people are very free with advice on the list (whether wanted or not) and can point you in the right direction if you have problems finding a ¾ inch flux capacitor for your 1984 vintage submarine.

Navigation and related announcements

If you would like to keep up to speed with announcements, news, and press releases from the IWAI, you can subscribe to the association's news updates list at **www.iwai.ie**

THE ROYAL CANAL AMENITY GROUP

Formed as a local organisation in 1974, the original objective of the RCAG was to promote and participate in the development of the full amenity potential of the Royal Canal in County Dublin. From these small beginnings the group continued to grow and now has a membership of approximately 500. It was not long before the group's activities extended eastwards into the City and westwards into Kildare and Meath, and very soon it had assumed 'responsibility' for the whole canal. The formation of local branches was encouraged; the first in Ballynacargy & Abbeyshrule, then in Kilcock, Enfield, Killucan, Maynooth, Mullingar, Longwood, Keenagh & Foigha, Killashee, Ballymahon, Longford, Cloondara, Coolnahay and Hill of Down. All these branches work closely with community councils or residents associations to develop local stretches of the waterway.

Much of the group's work is done voluntarily by members, but it has also sponsored many Youth and Social Employment Schemes. One of the most successful of these was a joint RCAG/FAS project for the construction of new lock gates for the whole Dublin-Kildare-Meath stretch of the canal. The group, of course, works in close collaboration with the staff of Waterways Ireland who provide invaluable help and assistance.

Membership

Although, in the past, the RCAG has received financial assistance from local authorities and other bodies it is now almost entirely dependent upon membership subscriptions, donations and profits from fund-raising activities to meet the considerable costs involved. You may like to make a donation, or become a member of the group. Members receive newsletters and they have an opportunity to meet together at film shows, canal walks, boat rallies and other social events.

How to join

The Honorary Membership Secretary, Noel Spaine, 42 Martin Savage Park, Ashtown, Dublin 7. Tel: + 353 (0)1 838 7023 will be pleased to send you a membership application form and, if requested, the name and address of the Secretary of your nearest branch.

Activities

Further information on boat rallies and other activities is obtainable from the Honorary Secretary, Patrick Greene, Rathwire Lower, Killucan, Co. Westmeath. Tel: + 353 (0)44 937 4373.

NOTES

NOTES